W9-BXY-921

English # Heritage
Book of
Hadrian's Wall

English ⌗ Heritage
Book of
Hadrian's Wall

Stephen Johnson

B. T. Batsford Ltd/English Heritage
London

© Stephen Johnson 1989

First published 1989

Reprinted 1989

All rights reserved. No part of this publication
may be reproduced in any form or by any means,
without permission from the Publishers.
Typeset in Great Britain
by Lasertex Limited,
Longford Trading Estate,
Stretford, Manchester M32 0JT
and printed in Great Britain by
The Bath Press, Bath
for the Publishers, B.T. Batsford Ltd,
4 Fitzhardinge Street, London W1H 0AH

ISBN 0 7134 59573 (cased)
0 7134 59581 (limp)

Contents

Illustrations

Colour plates

Acknowledgements

In writing a book of this nature, it is impossible to begin without acknowledging a great debt to scholars who have researched into elements of the Wall and its structures. Many of their written works are listed in the 'Further reading' section, but I also owe a personal debt to many people currently engaged in work on the Wall. It is impossible to mention them all by name, but Paul Austen, Julian Bennett, Paul Bidwell, Mike Bishop, Jim Crow, John Dore, and Tony Wilmott have all at various times been especially helpful, whether they realised it or not, and several of them have unstintingly helped me to make the material in this book as up-to-date as possible. My time spent as the member of the Ancient Monuments Inspectorate with responsibilities for Hadrian's Wall between 1981 and 1986 brought me into contact with many people who had thought about the Wall and its problems extensively, and who knew (and know) far more about the Wall than I did (or do), and much of what is written in this book I owe unconsciously to them. This is not to claim that anyone other than myself is responsible for any mistakes which remain.

The views stated in this book, in particular as regards the implementation of policies for preservation and protection of the Wall and its landscape in Chapter 10, are those of the author. They cannot therefore be taken as official pronouncements on behalf of English Heritage on these issues.

For illustrative material I am especially indebted first to Frank Gardiner, of English Heritage's Publications Drawing Office, for all of the colour reconstructions of the Wall and its forts, as well as for most of the black-and-white reconstructions (figs 18, 28, 38, 42, 50, 65, 72 and 73). For the rest of the plans and drawings apart from colour plate 2 by Peter Conolly and fig 37, by David Neal, I am grateful to Andy Maclaren, from the same office.

For the use of photographs I wish to thank the following, who also hold the copyright:

Archaeological Unit for North-East England, figs 41, 55.
Bob Bewley, figs 25, 91 and colour plate 1.
Cambridge University Collection, figs 7, 47, 56, 58, 74, 75.
Carlisle Archaeological Unit (Dorothy Charlesworth collection), fig 8.
English Heritage Central Excavation Unit, figs 22, 83, 92.
Barri Jones, fig 13.
Department of Antiquities, Newcastle upon Tyne, figs 27, 31, 62.
Jim Crow and the National Trust, figs 21, 43, 93, 94.
Corbridge Museum, figs 15, 63, 68, 84, and colour plates 3, 4, and 5.
Tyne and Wear Museums, figs 67, 80, 97.

All other photographs, including the reconstruction drawings, come from the collections held by English Heritage.

I am grateful to Yim Lam and particularly to Sheila Mason for their considerable help in typing and preparing this book for publication.

London, July 1988

1

The Wall and its setting

By the time of Hadrian's accession as emperor of the Roman World in AD 117, the empire he controlled was vast. Centred around the entire Mediterranean Sea, it embraced the coastal plains of Africa, the desert lands of Spain and Egypt, and skirted the hills of Asia Minor and the fringes of the Caucasus. Across Europe, the empire stretched the full length of the Rhine and the Danube, took in the whole of what is now France and the Iberian peninsula as well as much of lowland Britain. At its peak under his predecessor Trajan, the area directly controlled by Rome, subject to its laws and taxes, and profiting from its coinage and economic opportunities stretched some 3000 by 1750 miles (4800 x 2800 km) from the Guadalquivir to the Gulf of Suez, from the Tigris to the Tyne.

An area so extensive encompassed what most Romans were content to call the 'known world'; although Rome's influence extended beyond these bounds for such things as trade in silks, spices and other luxuries, the internal economy was largely self-sufficient. Yet the Roman world had boundaries, some natural, some artificial. In Africa, for example, the coastal plains allowed settlement in an urbanised, controlled fashion with areas of concomitant settled agricultural exploitation. Desert tribes, however, who were used to a more nomadic existence, and to whom the movement of flocks and herds between feeding grounds was important, posed an insistent threat to the smooth patterns of organised life. Here the boundaries between those styles of life might overlap, and force the Roman authorities to impose artificial controls on nomads by means of frontier barriers. In mainland Europe too, tribes of farmer-warriors, living in conditions probably only marginally less comfortable than their Romanised counter-

parts inside the empire, might, when crops failed or when political necessity squeezed them, spill across to the Roman side of the river or of the fence. This would automatically produce problems of settlement of refugees, of potential damage to crops or to houses.

In the east too, Rome always had to be wary of the power of the Persian empire: Trajan's aggressive wars of conquest, which pushed the boundaries of Rome's power as far as Babylon and Ctesiphon, were largely abandoned by Hadrian. The power of Persia was for much of the Roman imperial period strong, and it was necessary to maintain peace in the east by diplomacy if not by conquest.

There were thus frontiers all around, to serve all sorts of purposes: to stake out territory and mark the boundaries, to act as a control on traffic and trade, to provide protection and greater security. Each frontier area faced different problems, which needed perhaps to be answered in different ways. Strategically, therefore, they were planned for different purposes, and no one of them should be regarded as totally typical. Perhaps it is ironic that Britain, which must be regarded as something of an offshoot from the main European Roman world, should contain one of today's best known Roman frontiers — Hadrian's Wall.

Statistically speaking, Hadrian's Wall (1) ought to be counted as one of the wonders of the ancient world: it was a barrier, eventually of stone, running for 80 Roman or 73 British miles (117 km). It stood 7–10 ft (2.2–3.1 m) thick, and as much as 15–20 ft (4.65–6.2 m) high, festooned with regular towers and other installations for garrison troops. In terms of its construction alone, it was a massive undertaking — one that perhaps more than anything

1 *Hadrian's Wall at Walltown turret (no 45a): immediately beyond the turret the Wall has been quarried away, but its course is marked by the hills in the middle and the far distance. To the left, on the nearer skyline, the 'Nicks of Thirlwall', while in the middle, and more distant, Winshields. Over all these hills, the Wall clings to the forward edge, using the sheer face to the north as added protection.*

else helps to substantiate our own conceptions about the grandeur of the Roman world.

In the ancient world, however, long walls of themselves are not unknown: more famous than Hadrian's Wall is the great wall of China, in origin a series of border defences which were amalgamated into a coherent defence some 300 years before Hadrian. Even earlier were Greek Walls — the effort to block off the narrow isthmus of the Peloponnese against the Dorian invasion, and other defences for elements of the Greek mainland. Hadrian's Wall, however is

different: it is a strategic attempt to control a large tract of territory which has no obvious military coherence. Its very construction — whether it successfully performed its required function or not — is a grandiose concept. It was a mark of power, and displayed a consistency of planning and a thoroughness of execution, combined with a technical grasp of landscape control whose overall scale is hard to parallel in Britain until the cutting of the network of canals in the late eighteenth or the planning of the railways in the early nineteenth century.

The landscape of the British Isles can change relatively rapidly from area to area. In planning its course across northern England from the mouth of the Tyne to the Solway Firth, the Wall's builders had to contend with several contrasting zones: the gently undulating slopes of the fringes of the Tyne valley, the ascent on to the great granite outcrop of the Whin Sill, then the gradual descent along the softer sandstone ridges down to the flatter land of the Solway coast. Between the two coasts the Wall has to cross three major rivers as well as adapt itself to the contrasting terrain. Not all the land allows technical or military considerations to be taken easily into account, but the Wall takes tactical advantage of its siting wherever possible. The problems presented by its position seem to modern eyes to be ably answered, though of course we can only deduce from its present appearance precisely what strategic considerations were uppermost in the Romans' minds. There is no mistaking its planners' grasp of the terrain; the impression caused by the Wall's snaking, almost relentless, course across low and high land, is immediate and striking.

But it is not only this that makes the Wall so appealing. No other frontier zone of the Roman world contains such a wealth and complexity of Roman remains. The area on which these sites were planted is a broad and extensive landscape covering much of northern England and southern Scotland, for Hadrian's Wall is not an isolated phenomenon. It is a part, albeit one of the more lasting and substantial ones, of a framework of Roman military occupation, which for over 300 years saw this whole tract

of northern Britain as a frontier zone. Within this area, the marks of conquest and control, of retrenchment and defence, of aggression or conciliation can still be traced — sometimes blurred and sometimes starkly clear — in the modern landscape.

The Wall stands proudly as part of the evidence for this episode of history, played out by combatants long dead. They have left their record implanted on the landscape in the shape of forts, camps, settlements, roads and all the military paraphernalia of Rome. Their memory remains, too, in more personal ways — in religious dedications on tombstones, in finds of personal equipment of belongings, or sometimes even in their letters — all of which can illuminate for us what it was like to be assigned a Roman frontier posting in the Wall zone.

For today's visitor, the opportunity to come

2 *The Roman milestone beside the Stanegate at Chesterholm. Although the stone bears no visible inscription, it is one of a series placed along the Roman road in this area, and appears to mark a point 15 miles from Corbridge.*

close through these means to people of 1800 years ago and more is an important factor in our attempts to understand the past. No matter how much we may be able to empathise with individuals whose records still by chance remain, the concentration of Roman elements within the present-day landscape leaves the most striking impression. Nowhere does the Wall survive to its full height, but even so, in the central section where it climbs the ridges of the Whin Sill which present their rugged, sometimes sheer face to the north, the picturesque combination of these crags with the

ancient remains is at its most evocative. Eighteenth-century landscape gardeners who fashioned artificial parklands round a real or a mock ancient ruin to create a perfect backdrop could hardly have achieved a better blend of art and nature than this. Yet here the Wall and its landscape — or rather, the other way round — goes on for miles. Moulded and softened by time, but still the creation of the uncompromising terrain, the Roman element is often subtle and has to be looked for. Archaeology and landscape are here in delicate balance: ultimately, both are the product of man's activity, and it is therefore sometimes hard to tell where one finishes and the other begins.

Roman elements are to be seen all around. The Wall, even where it passes through conurbations at each end, can still be recognised in places. Its ditch, its accompanying earthworks, its roads and forts can still be traced by a roll in the ground, a dip in the hedgerow, a parched line in summer, or as a series of significant

3 *The temple of Antenociticus, Benwell. This was discovered in 1862, when the two altars, now represented on the site by casts, were found. They were dedicated by a centurion of the twentieth legion and by a man who was quaestor designate, in AD 179 or 180. From the site also came the head of the god's statue (62).*

bumps in a field, even in those places where there are no obvious stonework remains standing above ground. At Chesterholm, a Roman milestone still stands in position to prove that the farm track it stands by is really the Roman Stanegate (2); at Benwell, all but swamped by a housing estate, foundations of a tiny temple to a long-forgotten god are a reminder that this was once the settlement round the nearby fort (3). Elsewhere, the massive blocks of stone which still block the Wall ditch are a reminder that even the determination of Roman masons had sometimes to give way to the sheer difficulties of forcing the Wall through solid granite terrain. Graffiti left by men on quarry duty while cutting stone for the Wall — 'this is Flavius Carantinus' rock' — reveal that the apparent need felt by people everywhere to record their presence, particularly when the work is boring or frustrating, is not confined to our present age (4).

This richness and diversity of Roman remains is hard to parallel elsewhere: the traces of Rome are clearly visible in the desert areas of Africa or the Middle East, but they are neither as concentrated nor as immediately appreciable. A great deal of work has been done on the German frontier, and there are some spectacular sites — among them Saalburg, or the new archaeological park at Buch — but the signs of the frontier are not so obvious, nor do they involve as many different remains — forts, temples, settlements, marching camps and bathhouses, as well as frontier works themselves — as can be seen on Hadrian's Wall. Indeed, this concentration of identifiable and visible remains written on to the landscape imparts an historic identity to the Wall area as surely as does a cluster of well-loved distinctive buildings to one of our historic towns.

This is a cultural resource which we have to nurture carefully. Over-exploitation either of the archaeology or of the considerable wildlife could easily lead to damage. The archaeological resource, though large, is finite: in order properly to be understood, sites have to be examined thoroughly and once only. There is no point in half-measures, and a site once excavated cannot

4 *The rock-cut inscription from the Roman quarry at Fallowfield Fell, near Chollerford. The inscription reads PETRA FLAVI CARANTINI, 'the rock of Flavius Carantinus'*

easily be reinterpreted. In addition, any exposure of Roman remains to the ravages of the weather is likely to accelerate its decay. Consolidation and display of parts of the Wall for public view and enjoyment is a time-consuming and expensive business. It takes much concentrated work to allow this seemingly natural landscape to remain in good condition, to ensure that the Roman elements within it are recognised, appreciated and protected from damage, and to ensure, too, that all other interests — those of wildlife conservation, of estate management, of education and, perhaps most important of all, of the farmers who make their living from the land — form a harmonious amalgam.

A landscape rarely stands still: it bears the imprint of the past, but if it is to thrive it has to absorb the reasonable pressures of the present. Those who live and work in the Wall area, visit it, research into its Roman history and archaeology, or are involved in any way in its care and management bear a heavy responsibility in ensuring that its quintessential elements are preserved today and for the future. Fundamental to this is the need to understand the remains it contains, in order to appreciate what deserves our attention. It is possible then to take steps both to display them to the discerning visitor and to ensure that they are protected as best we can from the pressures of the present.

2

The build-up to the Wall

Roman forces arrived decisively in Britain in AD 43. Claudius, one of the only surviving members of the Julio-Claudian imperial dynasty and universally ignored because he was thought unfit for power, had, almost by accident, become emperor. Political pretexts, the need to support established allies, and the desire to gain credibility at home conspired together in his formulation of a plan to invade Britain. The power of the Roman armies now consolidating their hold on the lower Rhine, combined with Claudius' efforts to encourage the adoption of Roman customs, administrative systems, and laws in the remainder of Gaul made it possible to think once again of expansion. Britain was, however, to some extent an unknown land — it lay beyond the sea. Only three years previously, troops had mutinied rather than cross to Britain on the previous emperor Caligula's orders. This time, however, planning and personnel were adequate, and the troops responded with their loyalty.

Britain at the time was the home of a number of independent and self-contained tribal units, each ruled or controlled by its own aristocracy. Some already had links with Rome through treaties of friendship, through diplomacy, or through trade, and therefore welcomed or even encouraged her intervention. Others, perhaps seeking to broaden their own power base among the British tribes, were violently opposed to it. After the initial skirmishes, however, the gradual war of attrition and the constant pressure Rome could apply through her professional army began to take its effect, primarily in the south-east. Celtic tribes could not maintain a standing army, and many tribes therefore sought for peace or swore allegiance to Rome. Romanisation — the missionary process in which Rome concentrated on converting the tribal elite into the magistrates and elders of Roman cities — was set on its inexorable course.

The process was slow, to be sure, but effective. Within twenty years, where the Britons were receptive to Roman ideas and to the 'improved' way of life, the planting of new towns was nurtured at places like Silchester, London, and Winchester, though it was to be some time yet before they were provided with the full panoply of Roman-style buildings. Elsewhere, for example at Colchester, where loyalty could not perhaps be so readily assured, and where the processes of persuasion had to be more forceful, military sites might give way initially to colonies of veteran soldiers. Such sites as these, planted on British soil, would gradually soften into Roman towns comparable with the others, except in terms of their municipal status, as the first or second generations grew up. The process was quicker in the south-east than elsewhere; at places like Lincoln, Gloucester and Exeter it was to be forty years or more before the settlements attached to the early Roman military establishments developed into civilian towns, and much of Britain outside the south-eastern corner was still under military control into the AD 80s or 90s.

There were setbacks. One of these was the episode of Boudica's revolt in AD 60. By the late AD 70s, however, thirty-five or so years after their arrival in Britain, the Roman armies were based at Chester and at York facing north Wales and the north of Britain. Much of lowland England would pose no further problems: the aristocratic hierarchy of Celtic tribes was perpetuated in the divisive Roman class system and the tribes' historic areas of territorial control were readily translated into Roman administrative areas. A measure of self-determination was offered: the chance to serve and hold public office, to become a Roman citizen, to run the city's affairs; but there was also a measure of duty, loyalty and, of course, taxation. Markets began to open up for luxury goods, and the incentive to produce and become part of a thriving, organised economy was there for all to see and some — mainly only the chiefs or the craftsmen — to profit from. This was the picture in the south: for the north, things were different.

Here the Brigantes, whose tribal territory was spread over much of the north of England and parts of southern Scotland, presented problems to the Roman military forces. The tribe seems to have been a loose-knit confederacy of individual units which might have formed separate clan allegiances within the overall tribal structure. It was probably therefore less politically stable than many of its southern neighbours who had a well-defined class and nobility structure. Archaeological evidence shows the existence in the north for much of the late Iron Age and early Roman period of small scattered farmsteads, with only a small but growing amount of evidence for settled agriculture. There are very few obvious concentrations of settlement in hill forts in the area, and the evidence overall points to the existence here of mainly pastoral folk. Each local group — probably a family — might have been fiercely independent. The formation of political alliances may have been a continually shifting pattern and only concentrated in a common cause if there were strong coercive leadership.

Up until AD 69–70 the Brigantes had been considered one of Rome's client territories under their ruling monarch, Cartimandua. She had proved her loyalty to Rome in AD 51, when she surrendered Caratacus, whom the Romans considered a dissident, who had sought asylum with her, and on whom much of British resistance to the initial stages of the conquest had been focussed. Either now or for the future, this stored up internal political problems, and her husband Venutius, who did not share her compromised stance, appears to have been waiting his moment to concentrate anti-Roman feeling yet again. While Rome appeared militarily strong, he was forced to wait, but in 69, when the Roman world appeared in some turmoil, with loyalties distracted in internal struggles between emperors vying for power at the head of their rival troops, he judged the moment to be right for challenging Cartimandua's power, and for providing a focus once again for the opposition to Rome still latent in the north.

Decisive intervention on her behalf was not immediately practicable, whether because of temporary Roman military weakness or poor tactical sense on the part of the governor. When a new governor, Cerialis, appeared in AD 71, Venutius was now at the head of the Brigantes and posed a substantial and open military threat. To Cerialis is usually assigned the foundation of the legionary fortress at York, and from this base for the ninth legion, his forces probed steadily into Brigantian territory.

The site of the final battle and defeat of Venutius has normally, since Wheeler's imaginative combination of archaeological observation and historical narrative, been placed at the large earthwork enclosure round Stanwick, near Scotch Corner. According to Wheeler's view, a defended nucleus of about 16 acres (6½ ha) founded around AD 50 was extended on two separate occasions until it enclosed a massive area of 607 acres (243 ha) for Venutius' collected tribe and army. Recent re-examination at Stanwick, however, has cast doubt on the validity of this link between archaeology and history: that Stanwick was probably Cartimandua's capital can be surmised from the quality and quantity of early Roman material found there: it need not have been the site of the final battle. Nor is it by any means certain that Wheeler's interpretation of the sequence of earthworks is correct. The outcome of the campaign, however, is clear: the Brigantes were brought under some sort of control, and by the mid-seventies it is probable that Roman armies were pressing into areas such as Carlisle and even southern Scotland, though there is no evidence as yet of permanent bases there at this date.

There was apparently no consolidated further push northwards until the appointment, in AD 78, of a new governor, Agricola, whose achievements both in Britain and elsewhere were recorded by his son-in-law Tacitus, one of the most trenchant of Roman historical writers. On arrival in Britain, he apparently wasted little time before in his first season of command consolidating the Roman hold on north Wales, and securing his flanks against potential attack from that direction.

Cerialis' campaign, within which Agricola had figured as a junior officer, had paved the way for the next advance northwards, and had aimed at continuing the successful process of absorption of the new province. Even so, Tacitus' record of Agricola's achievements is spectacular — even accepting the natural desire of a son-in-law to flatter his subject. In a series of six campaigns, Roman troops in substantial numbers pushed up to the Carlisle–Corbridge line, conquered peoples in the western lowlands of Scotland, moved up to the Forth–Clyde isthmus, confronted the Caledonii in their own homelands, and met and defeated them in a decisive battle at *Mons Graupius*. Wherever the sites of some of these momentous encounters lie — and there are sometimes several candidates — the outcome of the campaign was clear. The Romans were seeking to impose a stranglehold on southern Scotland, applying a military tourniquet at the foot of the highlands which would allow northern England to be

assimilated, absorbed and Romanised, just as much of southern England had been before.

Archaeologically, the effects of this rapid advance can be readily seen. A number of marching camps, of several sizes, have left their trace in the southern and eastern fringes of the Highlands. By around AD 85, however, much of southern Scotland was mapped out with a network of new roads and permanent forts for garrison troops. A new legionary base was begun on an ideal site at Inchtuthil, near Perth: new forts were placed to watch for trouble coming from the north through the main Scottish glens. Work was well in hand to hold down this new territory. The axis for supporting this operation was up the two main routes northwards along the east and west sides of the country from the legionary bases now well in reserve at Chester and York.

Traces of the arrival and of the infrastructure to support substantial forces have been recorded most clearly at Corbridge. Excavations about 1 km north-west of the Corbridge museum on the line of the A69 bypass round the village located the site of a large military encampment nearly 800 ft (around 250 m) in length, its ramparts of earth or turf, and its internal buildings of timber (5). Since only a narrow strip across this site was available for study as part of the roadworks, the full plan is not known, but the installation contained at least thirteen sheds or stores as well as a workshop and barracks, possibly for legionary troops or for a mixed garrison. Just a little to its south, the construc-

5 *The plan of the Agricolan supply-base, Corbridge. Only the portion of the site which was to be destroyed by the construction of the road was available for excavation and therefore although the size of the base from east to west was determined, it was not possible to be certain how large it was from north to south.*

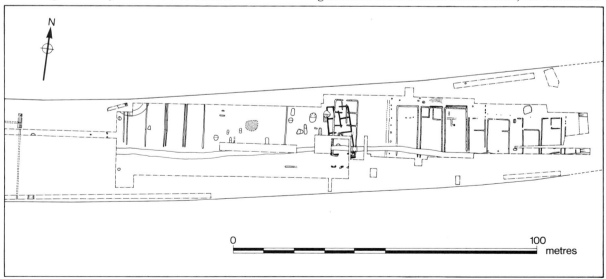

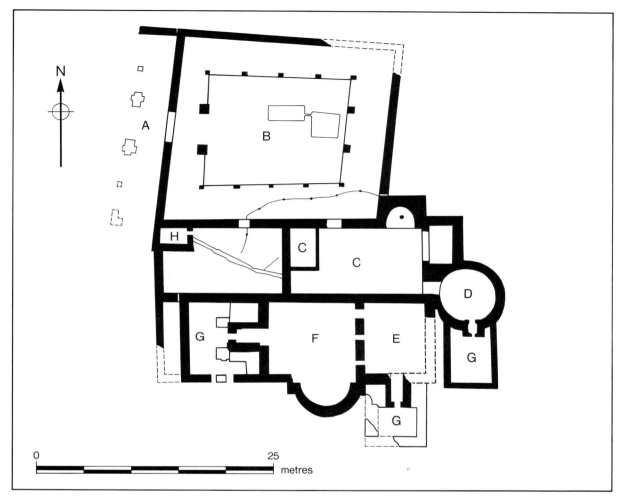

0   25 metres

tion of a substantial bath-building in stone (**6**), to a plan which is similar to other legionary baths, suggests that the troops stationed at this supply-base — for such surely it was — expected to be there for some time to provide logistical support. There seems little doubt that this base and its baths were established around AD 80 as part of Agricola's campaigns, and that there was some confidence that the Roman presence here would be permanent or at least long lived.

The pattern of establishment of forts in lowland Scotland at this date is a complex one, and allows only hints of the political situation at the time. There were two main routes into Scotland; the eastern, more direct one, from Corbridge, now followed by the A68 past the newly planted forts of High Rochester and Newstead (**7**), and the western one from Carlisle,

6 *The baths-building at Red House, Corbridge. This was a large and impressive building, with an entrance at A, a courtyard for exercise at B, and a series of bathing-rooms: cold baths at C, and warm and hot rooms at D, E and F. The small room at H is a latrine. The hot rooms were stoked by furnaces marked as G.*

aiming in the direction of Milton and Dalswinton. The number of Roman garrisons studding this area by the AD 80s suggests that there was a feeling that some areas of Scotland might still prove hostile to the Roman presence.

The provision was watchful and perhaps to some extent prophetic for, by 87, the situation was already changing. Military pressures elsewhere in the empire were a constant drain on the relatively limited Roman army resources,

7 *Cropmarks of the Roman fort at Newstead, in lowland Scotland. The site has four superimposed forts, the first of which was occupied from around AD 80–6, the second up to about AD 100, and others of second century date. This view shows the outline of the fort and some of its internal buildings showing clearly in the crop, as well as a number of other annexes and ditch systems in the nearby fields.*

and a legion (the *II Adiutrix*) was withdrawn from the British province. This left a weak infrastructure to support such a distended northern zone of operations, and dangerously exposed the legion *XX Valeria Victrix* still engaged in constructing the new fortress at Inchtuthil. When this legion was recalled to Chester, it must have already been clear that the territory gained by Agricola up to the fringes of the Highlands might have to be given up. It was only a question of when.

It may be at about this moment that more permanent bases were established at Carlisle and Corbridge. At Carlisle it is now certain that the Roman fort of this period occupied the site of the present castle: excavations near the museum have located and identified the substantial timber remains of its south gate

and turf rampart (8). In a confined working space, and in separate campaigns of excavation, little of the internal buildings could be examined, but the well-preserved remains of the rampart, ovens and workshops associated with it, were found in a remarkably fine state of preservation.

At Corbridge, the timber supply base established by Agricola was demolished, and replaced by a turf and timber fort of more regular auxiliary shape and size on the site now occupied by the present museum and its accompanying remains of later Roman buildings. This new site was well chosen, for the fort lay on a terrace just above the River Tyne where it could provide protection for the road which we know as Dere Street and control the point where it crosses the river. Traces of a bridge at this point at Corbridge have been located in the past in the river bed: a series of ten stone piers carried the road across the river. Recent research has suggested that, as they stand, these remains are of later date, but there must at this time have been at Corbridge a bridge with a wooden superstructure, similar probably to other contemporary bridges in other parts of the north, including Piercebridge. There was almost certainly a similar river crossing of

8 *A view from within the fort of the south gateway of the fort at Carlisle, founded around* AD *79, and excavated in 1978. The ranging pole rests against the central post which separated the carriageways through the gate, and one of the run-in slots for the gate can be seen just to its left. In front of the threshold is a wood-lined drain. Parts of the gate structure and of the turf fort ramparts can be seen top right. The mass of material top left is formed of layers of silt or mud associated with the abandonment of the fort.*

the river Eden by the Roman route running northwards along the western side of the country. This was overlooked by the fort at Carlisle, whose siting was in many respects similar to that of Corbridge.

Traces of this early turf and timber fort at Corbridge, and of a series of at least five other fort layouts which followed it on the same site, each slightly altering in internal plan though normally retaining the same overall shape within broadly unaltered ramparts and ditches, are buried deep under the visible stone remains on the Corbridge site (9). Nothing of the earliest fort, established in about AD 87, can be seen on the site today.

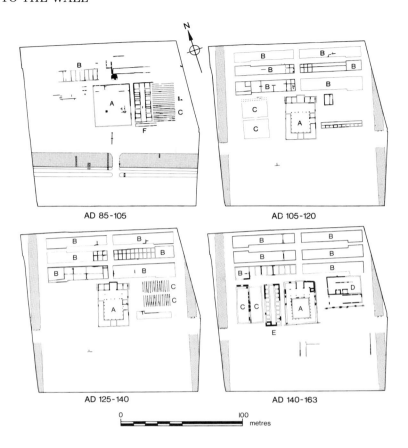

AD 85-105

AD 105-120

AD 125-140

AD 140-163

0   100
                        metres

9 *Four phases of the early fort plans beneath Corbridge Roman site; apart from the earliest phase, where it was not possible to be certain, these shared virtually the same internal area, but their layout was subject to continual changes. The following key is used to denote the uses of specific buildings within the plans: (A) head-quarters; (B) barracks; (C) granaries; (D) Com-mandant's house; (E) hospital; (F) workshop.*

One of the most impressive military tombstones from the region, now in Hexham Abbey, commemorates the death of Flavinus, a standard bearer of the *Ala Petriana* (a cavalry unit), and portrays him dressed in his full uniform riding down an unfortunate barbarian, perhaps a Brigantian, tribesman (**10**). Although the stone is rather worn, it shows Flavinus wearing a helmet crowned by an elaborate plume of feathers, clad in chain mail, and carry-ing a shield, sword and a staff which bears a portrait bust surrounded by a 'starburst'. From the evidence of its lettering and the dress it por-

trays, this stone is of late first century date, and its presence at Hexham suggests that it, like other material found at the Abbey, was taken here from the nearest available Roman site — of Corbridge. Thus Flavinus and his unit, the *Ala Petriana*, was probably stationed here, and shows that the garrison of this early fort was of cavalry.

Excavation at the Corbridge site over many years has now been able to clarify many details of the sequence of forts at the site. The initial layout clearly crystallised the shape and form of its successors: the western rampart lay pre-cisely beneath the present site museum, whereas the other three sides all lay beyond the limits of the site which is currently displayed to public view. Examination of the central range of the early fort has located its headquarters, rather larger than those of succeeding forts which may have been built for different units, as well as other buildings, including the distinctive parallel beam trenches which supported post-built granaries. Discolorations in the soil, mark-

20

ing the site of beamslots or trenches which once contained beams supporting posts for walls and other structural elements, are the only traces of these early forts which have been identified. They are buried deep under all the other remains on the site, and the difficulty of examining them has meant that the unravelling

10 *The tombstone of the Roman cavalryman Flavinus, of the* Ala Petriana. *He was the standard-bearer of the Unit, and his tombstone shows him in full regalia riding down a barbarian enemy. It can now be seen in the north transept of Hexham Abbey. The inscription records that he was 25 years old when he died, and had completed seven years of service.*

of the site's early history has been fearfully complex. In a series of research excavations carried out over more than thirty years, complicated by the difficulties of having to work in and around existing later Roman masonry buildings, the history of the Corbridge forts has been painstakingly pieced together. The results, though still fragmentary, will not be bettered by further work unless a greater area for research and excavation becomes available.

The Roman withdrawal from Scotland was carried out in a planned fashion (**11**). It may have been done in the face of insistent hostile pressure from Scottish tribes, with the initial abandonment of the zone north of the Forth–Clyde isthmus, followed by more gradual retrenchment elsewhere. These troops had to go somewhere, and there are signs that sites in northern England, in particular those in the Lake District and the Pennine area, were now being firmly established as the network of routes and garrison bases took shape. The withdrawal seems to have had the effect of heightening the importance of the cross-country link established between the forts at Carlisle and Corbridge, and one of the areas where it appears some new posts were created was on this road, which we know today as the Stanegate (**12**).

Because of the limited amount of research which has been done at some of the fort sites known to be on or near the Stanegate, it is difficult to be absolutely precise about which forts belong to the 80s or 90s, and which to the first or second decades of the second century. An early site is likely to lie at Carvoran, where aerial photographs show that the earthwork remains of the fort associated with Hadrian's Wall is a reduction in size from an earlier installation. Similar evidence also shows a larger and a reduced fort at another site, Nether Denton, though at both sites there is no indication of date of either the original fort or the smaller one which followed it.

It is clear, however, that a fort at Vindolanda was established in the 80s or 90s. Buried deep underneath the present remains, which belong to later periods, the traces of a large turf and timber fort, which may even have been founded by Agricola, have here and there been encountered. In one area, just outside the south-west corner of the later fort, deep excavations located waterlogged deposits, and led to the discovery of substantial numbers of finds of leather, wood

11 *Roman troop withdrawals from Scotland, AD 80–105. Most of the forts north of the line between Corbridge and Carlisle, known to have been established in the later decades of the first century (above), had been abandoned by AD 105 (below).*

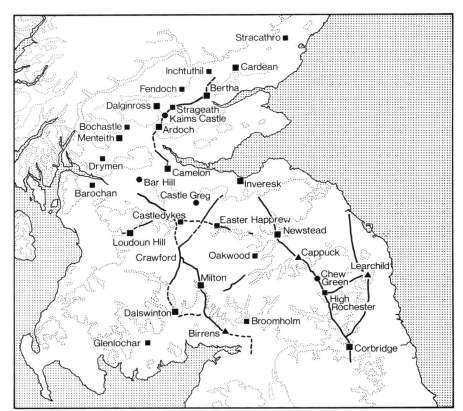

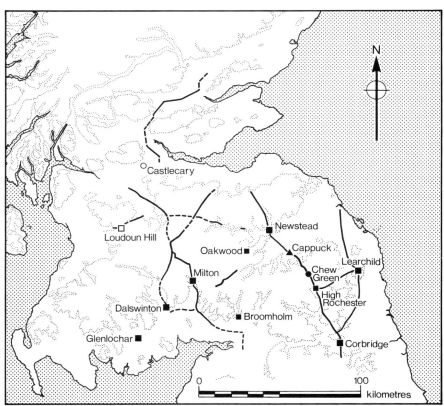

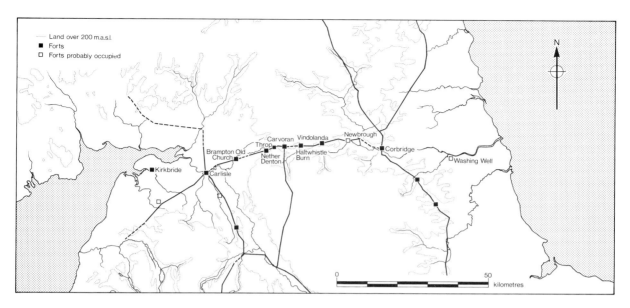

and other organic materials. They were found within and around a timber building which has been identified as the Commander's house of this early fort. The quality and quantity of this material gives a glimpse of what may have been lost at other sites where the conditions have not been so beneficial. There was a large amount of animal bone, wooden implements, and textiles. More than 200 shoes or portions of them, in various styles and sizes (some surprisingly small, and possibly for women or children rather than troops), were found. These, together with a considerable amount of offcuts and other pieces show that the process of tanning had been undertaken nearby — perhaps in an internal workshop.

The most exciting finds of all, however, were those of wooden writing tablets. Although over 400 of these have now been found, not all have yet been deciphered, and some of them may never have borne any writing. They come in two types: as flat tablets with a recessed central portion to take a thin skim of wax which could be written on with a metal stylus; or as wafer-thin sheets of limewood bearing writing in a carbon-based ink. Special techniques of excavation, careful handling, and photography by infra-red techniques had to be employed before much of what was written on the tablets could be deciphered. Roman handwriting is not always as neat as might be desired, and there are many examples within the Vindolanda tablets of variant spellings and some new

12 *The Stanegate and its forts. The map clearly shows the lack of known Roman sites east of Corbridge, and the dispositions west of Carlisle are still tentative.*

words — clearly military technical terms or other common usages — where the meaning is not entirely obvious. Some of the tablets are very fragmentary, and this has also made decipherment a painstaking process.

The tablets can now be seen to come from three separate deposits within the fort; they date from the years AD 90–100, between 100–05 and then down to 120. They appear to form an archive of official reports, records of supplies and stores issued or requested, as well as a series of letters, some of which are those written to the occupants of the fort and others apparently file-copies of those sent out. Among the historical pointers that the tablets give is the name of the provincial governor Neratius Marcellus, who is known to have been governor of Britain in 101–3, as well as the name of the fort's commander at the time, the *praefectus cohortis* Flavius Cerialis. The tablets certainly mention the presence at Vindolanda of both the third and the ninth cohort of Batavians, and it seems likely that the eighth cohort may have been there as well, probably between AD 100–05.

The official reports include a long five-page report on payments made '*ad sacrum*' — to the regimental strong room — and a list of foods supplied at the fort for a brief period in June

23

(the year is of course not known), which includes several different types of meat as well as barley, corn, wines, beer and goat's milk, and which therefore gives a great deal of evidence about the variety of the Roman soldier's diet. Its findspot, however, in the camp commandant's house could lead one to believe that it is a record of supplies for the commandant's household use alone. Other documents are duty rosters, cash accounts — including one which appears to show 'returns to the fort', perhaps from the sale of surplus materials to outsiders — and records of supplies or stock issued. One of these gives a list of a number of wooden items — spare parts used in the manufacture of carts — being sent out from Vindolanda.

One official report, quite short, but enormously informative about the way the Romans considered their adversaries and about the constant danger that they were in reads:

'... the Britons are unprotected by armour. There are very many cavalry. The cavalry do not use swords nor do the wretched Britons take up fixed positions in order to throw their javelins.'

From this alone, one can gather some of the frustrations of being posted on duty in the north, where the enemy are light, mobile and refuse to fight in the Roman cavalry fashion. The word for 'wretched Britons' — Brittunculi — unknown elsewhere suggests annoyance at their tactics.

Letters within the archive, like many other such documents, are hardly literary masterpieces. One, however, is of great interest since it serves to show quite vividly what Roman life was like in what must have been considered a military zone. It is a letter from Claudia Severa, probably the wife of the commander of a nearby fort, to Sulpicia Lepidina, who must have been the wife of Vindolanda's commandant, Flavius Cerialis. The letter invites Lepidina to her birthday celebration on 9 September and sends regards from her and her husband and her little son. The letter, part of it written apparently in Severa's own hand, conjures up a vivid picture of the social round of commandants' wives stuck in faraway Britain on military service, who, amid all the workaday concerns of camp life, could find the time to travel in what must have been fairly hostile terrain to celebrate a birthday party.

The dangers inherent in a spell of duty in the north at this time should not be underestimated. Archaeological finds suggest that, while withdrawals from Scotland were occurring from the late 80s onwards, around 105 a disastrous raid, which may have resulted in destruction at a series of forts including Newstead and Corbridge, meant that the Roman horns were drawn in even more tightly. Such evidence is always slightly equivocal. The Romans themselves would often demolish and even burn anything which could not be salvaged from their own forts on abandonment and the archaeological record rarely indicates whether those who carried out such destruction were friends or foes. At Newstead, however, a large cache of damaged parade-armour as well as indications that there were human victims of the onslaught, suggests that the destruction could be interpreted as the result of enemy action or as deliberate dismantlement. Similar traces of destruction at a number of other forts in lowland Scotland lead to the picture that there was now a concentration of Roman forces along the Carlisle–Corbridge axis and in the Pennines to the south. Few posts, if any, survived north of this line. The 'Brittunculi' were clearly making their presence felt.

Trajan had become emperor in AD 97, and the main problems he faced within the empire were clearly concentrated on other parts of the Roman world. Continued retrenchment in Britain may therefore have been partly a result of campaigns on others of the empire's boundaries, and in particular of his activities in Dacia (modern Romania) and in the East, where he adopted an aggressive stance towards the powerful Persian empire. Overall, at the time of his death in 117, the empire was at its fullest stretch: Roman armies had by now reached Babylon and into Transylvania, and had pushed out into the no-man's land between the rivers Rhine and Danube in mainland Europe. In those areas where expansion was not possible or practicable, importance was attached to consolidating gains and establishing fixed positions. In mainland Germany, this appears to have involved the clearance of a strip of territory to carry a track with observation towers — usually of timber with a small surrounding ditch — set out to guard and support the military cordon. Gradually this track — the latin name limes given to such a road has given us the word 'limit', signifying an 'edge' or a 'frontier' — became festooned with more

military installations. These included a number of small forts, each of them intended perhaps for no more than 150 men, which lay at points where access routes led into barbarian territories beyond. In places, larger forts were also added to the line.

It is tempting to look for traces of a similar scheme of Roman control within the Stanegate area between Carlisle and Corbridge at this same time. The Stanegate clearly did function as a lateral road, and the number of small and large posts along it was increased. It probably came to be regarded as a frontier only very slowly, and only after its static nature over several decades had crystallised Roman tactics and military expectations in the area. Indications are that the road may now have been extended west from Carlisle to Kirkbride, a fort which lay on the Wampool estuary.

The exact details of the chronological sequence of Roman military control of this area are still unclear, but there are forts and smaller watchtowers — one of which apparently precedes the implantation of a fort — between

13 *Aerial view of the fort associated with the extension of the Stanegate at Burgh-by-Sands. The wide dark line of the fort ditch can be clearly seen on three of its sides: the fourth must lie within the field nearer the camera where it does not show in the different crop. Excavations near the break in the ditch and on the smaller circular crop-mark in the top right corner of the enclosure suggested that there was a circular ditched watchtower followed by a fort, both of second century date.*

there and Carlisle. The development of a network of installations linked to the lateral road in this area is complex, and may have been similar to the sort of changes to the military cordon which were being made in Germany. The area of Burgh-by-Sands for example is typical. Excavators have here identified a timber tower within a small ditched rampart which was succeeded by a fort with an annexe (**13**). Nearby, aerial photography has identified another fort, itself apparently of two phases. Pottery recovered from all the sites could be

25

assigned to the early second century, but it is not certain whether all these developments have to be fitted into the history of the area

prior to the construction, only about a mile (2 km) further north, of Hadrian's Wall and its associated forts in the 120s.

Across the centre of the country, the Stanegate gradually gathered more posts along its line. Forts are known at Carlisle, Brampton, Nether Denton, Carvoran, Vindolanda, Newbrough and Corbridge, all spaced on average about 6 miles (10 km) apart, and supported both by watchtowers and small fortlets. At the existing fort sites, there was considerable change, presumably consequent upon a continual merry-go-round of different postings similar to the one which saw two or three different units

14 *Plan of the fortlet at Haltwhistle Burn. It was excavated in 1907–9, and stands on a small hillock above the stream, guarding the point where the Stanegate crosses it. The site can also be seen on* **25** *and* **colour plate 1**. *The accommodation it comprised seems to be (A) officer's quarters; (B) barrack; (C) centurion's quarters; (D, E) store-building and yard; (F) headquarters; (G) is a paved area.*

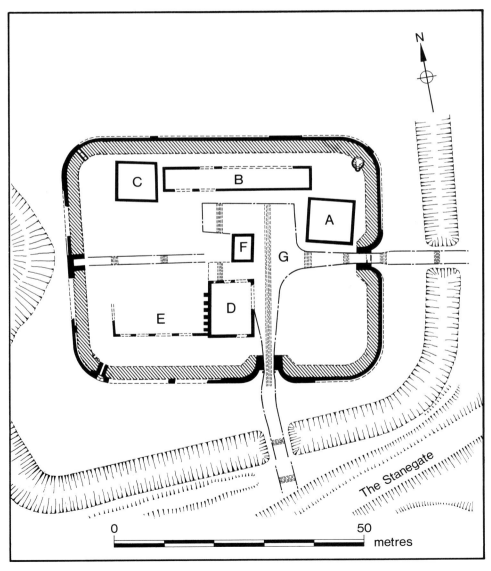

at Vindolanda between AD 90–120. At Carlisle, the internal buildings of the earlier fort seem to have been re-planned in the early part of the second century, and a building, probably a barrack block, replaced what had earlier been workshops. A pit within what had been the centurion's quarters within this building yielded a further group of writing tablets, though these have not yet been studied. Indications of a change in size of the fort at Nether Denton have also been noted, and at Corbridge where the fort destroyed in around 105 was re-planned, changes in garrison may have reduced its overall size as well as forced structural alterations to its internal buildings. A double undulation still visible across the southern part of the exposed remains at Corbridge could be the result of sinkage into an underlying double fort ditch. If so, these were not the main fort defences, but marked a temporary reduction in size of the fort (see **9**, p.20). As yet, however, it is not easy to see whether there was any extension of the military cordon from sea to sea, for the line of the Stanegate cannot be traced east of Corbridge, and only a single and unexplored fort, at Whickham, is known between it and the mouth of the Tyne. There almost certainly was activity here, for work at South Shields fort has revealed traces of a turf and timber fort underlying the present stone fort's remains.

The proliferation and establishment of new posts along the Stanegate line appears best to fit within the first two decades of the second century, and to form the kind of consolidation of the strategic position for which Trajan was responsible in Germany. One of the new installations on the Stanegate, the fortlet at Haltwhistle Burn, has been excavated (**14**). It was only about 210 x 170 ft (64 by 52 m) in size, with earthen ramparts given a stone facing. It lay within an irregular ditch, and contained at least one barrack, together with centurion's quarters, a store and part walled yard accompanying it, as well as a small administrative building. Other fortlets of similar size whose existence is known elsewhere along the line of the road may have had the same capacity, acting perhaps as the bases for small detached units to form the ears and eyes for the main troop units elsewhere.

Whether this concentration of activity in the area amounted to a realisation that this road was now the frontier is still unclear. With so much happening in other parts of the empire, a chance to rationalise in Britain in the face of hostility from the Scottish tribes was probably opportune. It would be foolish, however, to expect that the Roman military commanders of this date had it in mind to halt at the isthmus between Carlisle and Corbridge, or that they pinned all their hopes on a stable frontier along the Stanegate. Such solutions take a little time to mature, and, in any case, there was little collective experience in the Roman army of this date of retreat or of a totally static situation. The consolidation of the line of the Stanegate was probably more a response to pressure than the delineation of a frontier zone that was considered immediately to be tactically sound.

There are some signs that wars were still being fought and some pressure soaked up in Britain until the very end of Trajan's reign. Evidence comes from studying the careers of men who died in far-flung places, but who had previously won decorations for valour with troop units known to have been in Britain during Trajanic times: moreover one of the units later found on the wall — the earliest garrison at Chesters fort — was a cavalry unit which had been given the title 'Augusta' for its collective bravery. Such honours were relatively commonly awarded after outstanding service in battle, and the honour may have been won in action between AD 110–20.

Although the apparent mobility of the Roman forces in this northern zone at around this time is confusing, and its archaeological record often difficult to disentangle because of the layers of later Roman occupation on top of it, there have been some spectacular finds from this period, to add to those from Vindolanda described above. In 1915, just outside the fort of Carvoran a solid bronze corn measure in a truncated conical shape, now in the museum at Chesters fort, was discovered (**15**). This bears an inscription stating that it was made in the time of the emperor Domitian (AD 87–96), and that it officially contains $17\frac{1}{2}$ *sextarii*, or around 17 pints, of dry corn. In fact the measure holds 20 pints (9.7 litres) if filled to the brim, but it may have lost an internal gauge. It could have been used in the fort granary to check the weight of corn and other supplies by those whose business it was to record the delivery or issue of foodstuffs that we can see being recorded on the tablets from Vindolanda.

15 *The bronze corn-measure from Carvoran. The inscription certified the volume contained by the measure, together with the emperor Domitian's name. The erased patch in the top line of the inscription is all that is left of the emperor's name following the condemnation of Domitian's memory after his death.*

The constant alterations in fort garrisons, too, might lead to the abandonment of materials which it was not thought worth trying to salvage. In 1964, during excavations on the early forts at Corbridge, the remains of an iron-bound and leather-covered wooden chest were uncovered. This elegantly dovetailed box was found to contain a mixture of weapons and other implements, bundled up in cloth or tied with string (**colour plates 2,3**). It included at least six sets of segmental breastplates, folded up concertina-fashion, as well as a scabbard, ballista-bolts and spearheads. The mixed nature of the box's contents was confirmed by the fact that there were also saws, a crowbar and pulley-block, chisels and nails, as well as a wooden mug, a tankard and gaming counters. Analysis of the finds has shown that there were also writing tablets and possibly even feathers, along with textiles, within the group. The whole lot had been packed carefully within the box, and buried, perhaps around AD 120, or a little later, near a building which was probably a work-shop. Since many of the items in the 'hoard' were damaged, they probably formed the scrap-metal contents of the workshop which were assembled and buried for future use when the fort was evacuated by its unit. It is ironic that the modern study of this scrap metal, painstakingly carried out over several years, should have led to a significant advance in our knowledge of how the segmental breastplates functioned, and, for those with an interest in Roman armour at least, form one of the most significant groups of material found anywhere within the Roman world.

3

The Wall is begun

Trajan died on his way back from Antioch to Rome in AD 117, leaving Hadrian, then in the east, to claim the succession. At first there was some opposition, and initially the new emperor had to spend time in Rome improving his relationship with the Senate and securing his position. Only four years later, in 121, was he ready to examine in detail the military dispositions in the Roman world. As a serving soldier himself, he well understood the importance of stabilising the situation on the frontiers of the empire. From his experience under Trajan in the wars in the east, he will have gained a vivid impression of the practicalities of frontier control, and perhaps of the need to define what the Roman military could defend and what could be achieved through diplomacy. At any rate his biographer records that he abandoned some of the eastern provinces — those of Mesopotamia, Assyria, parts of Moesia and Armenia — which had been annexed and created by Trajan.

The same historian reveals something of Hadrian's nature when he records that in his tour of Gaul he took army discipline in hand. He established strict rules for soldiers' leave, stamped out some of the more comfortable aspects of military life and boosted morale by sharing personally in the troops' lifestyle, improving their equipment and their conditions and adjusting their length of service. The tour of inspection led him eventually from Gaul into Britain where he also carried out improvements and initiated a scheme for a wall to separate barbarians and Romans.

As with others of Hadrian's decisions which altered the state of affairs he had received from his predecessor Trajan, the proposal for a wall was a response to the military dispositions in

northern England up to about 120. As with the German frontier, which Hadrian later visited, it was not felt sufficient just to continue with a frontier track: something more permanent was required. In Germany, between the Rhine and Danube, a palisade was erected. In Britain, the existing Stanegate line was to be supplemented by a more massive wall.

The wall was planned to run, not in the generally lower-lying terrain favoured by the Stanegate road, but on higher ground normally to be found some short distance to the north of it (16). The wall maintained a reasonably close relationship with the road, but made the best use possible of strategically good ground which allowed a view northwards. Working from east to west, from central Newcastle, *Pons Aelius*, the site of the new bridge, where the Wall seems originally to have begun, the Wall strikes straight out just north of west following the crest of the rising ground on the north of the Tyne valley, normally no more than about 3 miles (5 km) north of the river. This relationship and the rough alignment, with slight adjustments between hill-tops, is maintained until the Wall drops down to cross the northern branch of the River Tyne at Chesters. Between Corbridge and Chesters, the Stanegate followed the valley of the river, but its course between Newcastle and Corbridge has not been discovered, though it may have been south of the River Tyne.

Beyond the crossing of the Tyne, however, both Wall and Stanegate branch out into more rugged territory. The Whin Sill, a fold of rock of volcanic origin, rises with a sheer northern face, often some 200 ft (60 m) high, and runs for about 10 miles (6 km) in the central section between the Tyne and the Solway estuaries. At this point, the valley of the South Tyne snakes

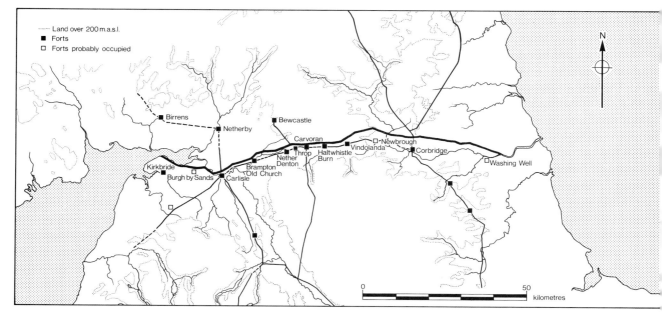

16 *Hadrian's Wall as originally planned. The main troop-bases remained those on the Stanegate, in some places well to the rear of the line taken by the Wall.*

away southwards (**colour plate 1**). The Wall uses the crags of the Whin Sill to best advantage, and the road, ever in its shadow, takes an easier route still some distance to the south. At Greenhead, as it descends from the main heights, the Stanegate and Wall virtually converge. For some miles they are separated by the River Irthing, and the Wall takes an aggressive stance to its north, while the road, still normally within sight of the Wall, once more follows lower ground in its valley to the south.

As it reaches Carlisle, the rugged landscape gently folds into the lower land on the shores of the Solway Firth. After crossing its third main river, the Eden, at Carlisle, the Wall follows the shoreline of the Solway Firth for 14 further miles — a stretch that encompasses all the known points of the Firth which could be forded in Roman times — until it dives into the sea near Bowness. The Wall was thus planned to be 76 Roman miles (111 km) long.

Archaeological traces of the Wall have added a great deal of detail to this outline design. The wall curtain itself was of stone between Newcastle and the crossing of the River Irthing — that is, for the eastern 45 miles —

with the remaining 31 miles (45 km) on the west constructed of turf. It seems to have been intended as a continuous barrier. In its stone-built portions a foundation was laid 10 feet (3 m) wide, intended, one might think, for a wall of similar width. In the event, however, the Wall was sometimes not completed to this specification, and in many places a narrower gauge wall stands on this broad initial foundation (**17**). Where the wall was of turf, it seems sometimes to have stood on the ground surface, and sometimes on a prepared platform of cobbles some 20 ft (6 m) wide. Its superstructure was of cut blocks of turf laid in courses.

From the beginning, the barrier was planned to comprise more than just a curtain wall. At regularly spaced intervals of about a mile along its length lay a small walled fortlet (**18**). These were attached to the southern side of the Wall, and though they vary in size and in external dimensions, they average about 60 ft (18 m) square internally. Their northern wall is formed by Hadrian's Wall itself, and most of them have a gateway leading through the Wall to the north, and were approached by a similar gate in their south sides. These 'milecastles' therefore were controlled crossing points through the Wall as well as affording a limited amount of space for a stable garrison. By modern convention, they are numbered from east to west: thus of those which can be visited, Sewingshields milecastle is the 35th from the

east end of the Wall, and the one at Poltross Burn, at Gilsland, the 48th. Where the milecastles were built as part of the turf wall, west of the River Irthing, their ramparts were of turf like the Wall to which they were attached.

Further structures were also planned to be integral with the wall. Between each pair of milecastles, the Wall's planners set two equally spaced towers which were thus approximately a third of a Roman mile apart (**colour plate 10**). These are known today as turrets, and they were of stone, albeit of slightly differing dimensions, whether originally planned for the stone wall or for the section first built in turf.

It is clear that a task such as the construction of the wall and all these component structures could not be undertaken immediately. It is fortunate therefore that a number of building records survive, both formal inscriptions recording construction of milecastles, and a number of smaller stones, normally set into the fabric of the wall, which marked the completion of sections of curtain walling by the detachment of troops assigned to a particular portion of the task. From these it can be deduced that the

17 *Hadrian's Wall at Planetrees. At this point there is a join between the completed Broad Wall (to the right of this picture) and the narrower gauge Wall to the left. In the foreground a culvert runs through the Wall, but immediately behind it is the point where the wall was reduced in width by about 2ft 4in (70cm).*

work of building the wall was entrusted to legionary troops to organise and execute. The building records show that three legions — *II Augusta, XX Valeria Victrix* and *legio VI Victrix* — took part in the wall's construction.

Detailed excavation and study of several of the milecastles and even more of the turrets have suggested that there are three separate types of each structure on the Wall (**19**). Variations in their wall-width, in their gate plans, and in the proportions of the dimensions indicate that three different blueprints for milecastles all apparently built around a similar module, were in use. A pair of inscriptions from milecastle 38, at Hotbank near Housesteads, shows that the type which is internally broader than it is deep was built by the *legio II* (**20**).

31

18 *A reconstructed milecastle — Cawfields. It may be that towers over the milecastle gateways were higher than those shown on the drawing. No trace of internal buildings has been recorded at Cawfields, and those shown here are therefore conjectural.*

Similarly, an inscription from milecastle 47 shows that the type of milecastle which is deeper than it is broad and with gateways with extended passageways was built by *legio XX*. A third type of milecastle, of similar overall shape to the last, but with a distinctively different gate plan, may have been the work of the *legio VI*.

Surprisingly few milecastles have been excavated under modern conditions, and only two have in recent years been thoroughly examined. At Sewingshields milecastle, one of the least hospitable points on the wall, excavation showed a remarkable sequence of buildings (see **81**, p. 107) which had begun in the Hadrianic phase with a simple single internal stone building set in the south-east corner. This was a two-roomed barrack, apparently the only accommodation within the enclosed area, a layout which is strikingly paralleled by milecastle 50 on the turf wall where a single building in

timber of precisely the same plan was encountered. That this plan was not necessarily a standard one, however, is suggested by work at milecastle 39, where the earliest layout appears to have been a single building — perhaps of timber on a stone dwarf wall — occupying one side of the milecastle with a veranda along the road through its centre. Here, as at Sewingshields, occupation was long-lived, and there were many alterations in the layout of its internal accommodation during the period during which the wall was occupied.

Despite there being little scope for variation, turrets also can be seen to have been built according to one of three different designs. These seem consistently to correspond with areas of the Wall which contain milecastles of one of the three particular plans and may also therefore be the product of individual legions' techniques. Thus turret 33b, with its door to the east, has produced an inscription of the sixth legion, though as this was found reused within the wall of the turret when it had been deliberately dismantled (in the third century?) it cannot be absolutely certain that the inscription either came originally from the turret or recorded its construction. Turrets with doorways to their west are found in the stretch of wall next to Poltross Burn milecastle and may therefore have been built by *legio XX*. This leaves the third type of turret, a square interior with slightly thicker walls, to be assigned to *legio II*.

From crumbs of evidence such as these, a pattern has been gradually built up to show that the three legions carved up the work in roughly equal lengths of about 5–6 miles (8–9.6 km) between them. If some of the detail is still sketchy, it is because the accuracy of evidence and observation about wall structures in the past has not always permitted firm

conclusions to be drawn: besides, our knowledge of wall structures and the amount of work which it has been possible to carry out on them is patchy. It might be expected that the Roman approach to building the Wall, particularly if

19 *Comparative plans of milecastles:* (A) *milecastle 9 (Chapel House), probably built by the sixth legion;* (B) *milecastle 42 (Cawfields), by the second legion;* (C) *milecastle 48 (Poltross Burn), by the twentieth legion;* (D) *the turf wall milecastle 50 (High House).*

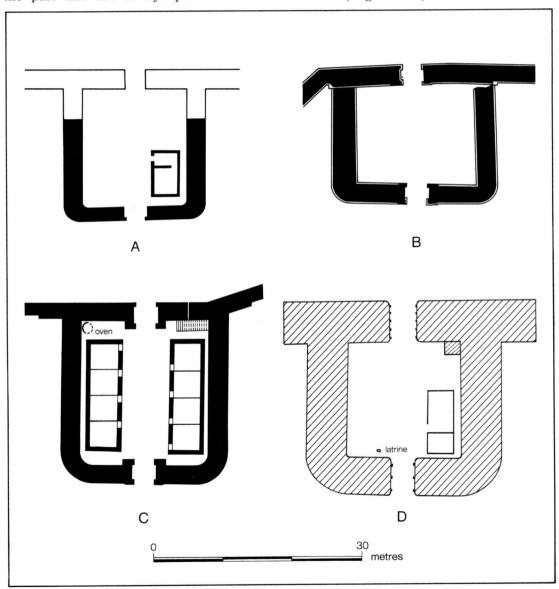

20 *One of the two building-inscriptions from Hotbank milecastle (no 38): It records its construction by the second legion in the reign of Hadrian under the governorship of Platorius Nepos.*

the three separate legions were involved, would be systematic and regular. The pattern which is emerging may be altered by new evidence, but as it stands, this interpretation feeds off the archaeological data about the Wall collected over several decades, and seeks to explain it.

There are further complexities. It is clear, for example, that although planned as a curtain wall 10 ft (3 m) thick, the actual barrier was not always completed to this width. Although in places it does measure the full 10 ft (3 m), in others it is nearer 8 and in still others only 6 ft (1.8 m) thick, as well as a number of intermediate dimensions.

The different widths to which the Wall was completed in different places have given rise to theories which suggest that the amount of stone required to complete the work planned and begun to the proposed ten-foot standard was excessive, and, for one reason or another, perhaps because of other alterations in plan which took place later, economies were set in train. Detailed excavation work in recent years on stretches of wall curtain, notably those near Steel Rigg in Wall mile 38–39, have shown just how complex the history of the Wall's construction really is. Although in many places the Broad Wall foundation was discovered at the foot of the existing wall, the width of

the wall that was eventually built on it was narrower, and was often of two or more phases. In one place, on the top of Highshields Crags, it was discovered that sufficient time had elapsed between the construction of the broad foundation and the building of the narrow Wall for a build-up of soil to have covered the foundations. Elsewhere, the broad wall foundation had not been used by the later narrow wall at all, and took quite a different line along the top of the crags (**21**): had it not been for medieval shielings nestling against the inner face of the Wall at this point which required examination, it is doubtful that the broad wall foundation would have been discovered by the excavators at all. The same campaign of work has also begun to identify a third phase of construction in the form of an even narrower wall, this time built or repaired in hard white mortar, which succeeded all the others. The dating of all these phases of construction still has to be determined, but this last phase of the Wall may not have been built until the third century. This leaves open the interesting possibility, still to be examined in detail, that parts of the original wall may never have been completed in the time of Hadrian at all.

The 10-foot (3 m) foundation however forms a base for much of the Wall's length, and seems to have served as a marking-out line to show the surveyed course it was to take. Not only that, but many of the milecastles and turrets were positioned, planned and at least partly built before the curtain was completed. Many of them have a short stub of wall of 10-ft thickness, to left and right intended from the first to facilitate the join between milecastle or turret and curtain wall, when the builders of the latter finally caught up. In the event, of course, when the main curtain wall was built to link these structures it was often of a narrower gauge, and consequently these small bonding walls did not need to be used to their full width. They do show, however, that the milecastles and turrets were built first and

21 *A view looking along a portion of the unused Broad Wall foundation located in excavation just east of milecastle 39. This rough foundation, no more than a single course deep, takes a different line along the top of the crags from that later followed by the Wall, and seems never to have been used to carry a superstructure. The buildings against the inner face of Hadrian's Wall in the middle distance are medieval sheilings.*

22 *The turf-wall foundation near Burgh-by-Sands. At this point, excavated in 1986, the turf wall was found to have been built in part on this cobble foundation, 19ft (5.8m) wide. When it was built, some time later, the stone wall was built on the same line in sandstone.*

incorporated in the continuous barrier later.

For the 30 or so miles of its length between the River Irthing crossing and the western end of the Wall at Bowness on the Solway Firth, the Wall was built not of stone but of turf. Roman forts and other encampments had traditionally been built of turf, and even now, by Hadrian's reign, stone was only gradually being introduced as a permanent building material for military structures. If the use of turf for this barrier seems unusual to us, therefore, it certainly was not so to the Romans themselves, and in their own view it was doubtless just as good as any wall of stone, at least in the short term. The reasons for the change of material are not altogether obvious. To be sure, there is a lack of good available building stone in north

Cumbria: the soft sandstones did not form ideal material, and better stone could only be had from further afield — from either the lowland Scottish zones or the Pennines to the south. In the shorter term, and as part of a project which required speedy implementation, the use of a traditional building method — turf and timber — will have seemed a ready, perhaps a preferable, alternative. Even when the frontier was pushed out further northwards some years later, the Antonine Wall was built in turf: on Hadrian's barrier it must have been stone which seemed anomalous. Turf, which could be easily cut locally and stacked so as to form a substantial obstacle, would have been ready to hand and economic of time and effort.

The same pattern, of milecastles and interleaved turrets, was maintained in this section of the Wall. The milecastles (**19**) had ramparts of turf. All these structures, including the Wall, stood on a broader base — up to 20 ft (6 m) wide, which in places might be founded on a footing course of cobblestones set in clay. Internal structures within the milecastles were of timber. The only buildings of stone were the turrets which were built without wing-walls as simple square towers. At a later stage, all the turf elements of this part of the Wall were converted to stone; the stone turrets were easily incorporated into the converted curtain, and the milecastles were completely rebuilt. Apart from one or two small stretches, the replacement wall followed the turf one almost exactly. Clear evidence of this was found in excavations near Burgh by Sands, where the later stone wall was found standing squarely on top of the prepared cobble footings for the turf wall (**22**).

As far as archaeological indications are concerned, the Wall, its milecastles and turrets, and, for most of its length, a substantial ditch to its north, was started relatively soon after Hadrian's visit to Britain which must have been in AD 122. Aulus Platorius Nepos, the governor named on the milecastle inscriptions as the man who oversaw the work, is known to have come to Britain from Germany where he was governor around 120 and to have succeeded Hadrian's first governor of Britain after his usual term of about five years. The evidence thus fits with the deduction that construction was well under way by late 122 and 123. Other

types of archaeological finds, coins, pottery and the like, can rarely supply a date as exact as the dates given by inscriptions: finds from the earliest levels of wall structures have produced nothing which can contradict this dating. The identification of structures belonging to the turf wall, west of the River Irthing, is less easy. Its remains are much more fragmentary, for it was later demolished for most of its length and replaced by the Romans themselves. Only one tiny chip of a primary inscription survives in this stretch: this is a small piece of wooden inscription from the turf-wall milecastle no 50. Despite its miniscule size, elements of Hadrian's name as well as that of Platorius Nepos are recognisable.

23 *The bridge abutment at Chesters from the north. Hadrian's Wall approaches the River Tyne from the left side of the picture, and the bridge crossed the river on a number of piers. The large masonry belongs to the large abutment of a bridge rebuilt in the third century. The Hadrianic bridge was less imposing (see **24**). Westward movement of the river has left all these remains now on the river's eastern bank.*

The Wall incorporated structures other than turrets and milecastles. At least two free-standing towers, already built, were incorporated within its course. One of these was turret 45a, which does not have the short tell-tale bonding stretches which would have been provided if it had been planned from the beginning as a turret, and the other was a signal tower at Pike Hill. This has a plan somewhat similar to a turret, but it stands at 45 degrees to the Wall's line and was built into its structure perhaps because it was in such a good observation position. Other towers associated with the Stanegate road and acting as lookout posts to guard the system of forts and communications lower down the valley may also have been added to the Wall at this time: alternatively, some of the better sited turrets on the Wall

could have provided ready-made forward look-out posts.

The other structures which were necessary were the Wall's three main bridges. Little is known of the bridge near Carlisle where the wall crosses the River Eden, but remains of the others are still to be seen at Willowford and at Chesters (**23**). At both places, despite considerable later rebuilding, mainly in response to changes in the courses of the two rivers they cross, elements of the Hadrianic bridges have been identified. At Chesters, a simple abutment was provided at the river bank for the Wall, which crossed the river on a series of eight hexagonal piers. The first of these from the east still survives where it was later incorporated into a larger abutment of third-century date, and shows that the piers were set about 13 ft (4 m) apart, with cutwaters both up and downstream. They were held together with dovetail clamps of iron set in lead to combat the force of the river. The alignment of the wall as it approaches the Chesters bridge from the east suggests that, as with wall structures elsewhere, the bridge may have been built before the remainder of the Wall was brought up to join it from the east and west. Its massive construction,

24 *Sketches of the Hadrianic and Severan bridges at Chesters. The Hadrianic bridge (A) was of the same width as the Wall, and carried it in stone across the river on eight piers. The Severan bridge (B), built around 207–208, sprang from a tower placed on a large abutment, and had only three river piers (see also* **colour plate 7**).

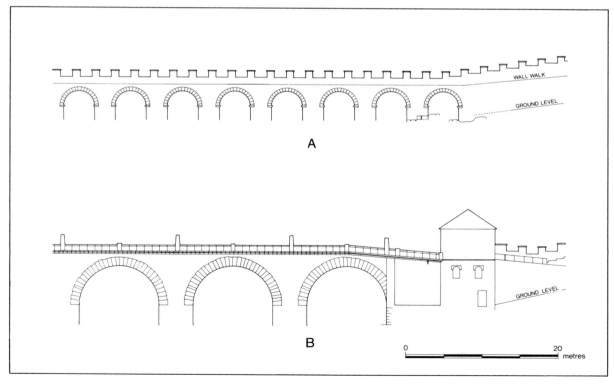

closely spaced piers, and the fact that the piers are of exactly the width to carry the Broad Wall suggest that the bridge was intended to carry the physical barrier of the Wall across the river: at only 10 ft (3 m) wide, with a stone superstructure, this cannot have carried anything other than a footbridge (**24a**).

The earliest bridge at Willowford was similar to the one at Chesters, though only fragmentary traces could be examined (**colour plate 6**). A large eastern abutment was associated with the end of the Wall, and the piers of the Hadrianic bridge. Scant enough trace of these had survived later rebuilding, but there were clear traces revealed by excavation of where the initial pier from the east had lain, and blocks with dovetailed cramp-holes, probably originally from these piers, are to be found in secondary use elsewhere in the structure. The discovery of a voussoir and a springer built into the later structure shows that the Hadrianic bridge was likely to have been of stone, not of timber, and like that at Chesters, carried the stone wall across the river. It, too, had been built before the curtain wall was brought up to it to incorporate it in the main structure.

For troops engaged in a project as massive as that of building the wall, one would expect there to be some sign of where the troops engaged in the construction work, organising corvées of builders, stonemasons and supplies, were actually housed. On the Antonine Wall, for example, built some few years later between the Forth and the Clyde, there are signs of the existence of temporary camps which can be relatively closely associated with lengths of the wall, constructed of turf, built by individual units. No such easy correlation, however, can be deduced from the remains of Roman temporary camps near Hadrian's Wall. Despite the fact that upwards of forty temporary camps of many different sizes, some of them still visible as earthworks, have been recorded in the vicinity of the wall, very few have been dated, and none can with confidence be found to have been occupied by troops engaged in construction (**25**). From our point of view, not only will a temporary camp, with a rampart of earth quickly thrown up around pitched tents leave little trace once abandoned, but it also can afford little prospect of significant archaeological deposits within its ramparts to define a date. Occupation of such an encampment will leave little trace. Unless it was more long-lasting and unless archaeologists of today locate rubbish deposits, the prospects for dating are slim.

We do not know precisely what size detachments of troops assigned to construction duties and camped together on the line of the Wall might have been: building inscriptions suggest that legions might be subdivided into centuries (of 80–100 men) or into cohorts (of 500 or so) for this work. A number of the smaller camps, usually identified as 'practice' camps thrown up by the army on manoeuvres, would have been of sufficient size to house small temporary detachments of these numbers of men. One camp, excavated because it was on the line of a new road near Corbridge, and apparently occupied for some years around AD 130, may have been a work camp overseeing nearby quarries. Others, in similar positions near known stone extraction sites, doubtless had a similar function.

Some of the sources of materials for the Wall have been located, partly due to the Roman soldiers' habit — perhaps a human reaction anywhere — of leaving their name carved on the quarry face. Thus, near Chollerford, a rock face bears the inscription 'Flavius Carantinus' rock' (see **4**, p. 13), and at the Cumberland end of the Wall, near Brampton, a vexillation of the second legion left an inscription to show they extracted stone, though they also left the consular date showing that this was not till the year 207 (see **76**, p. 102). Other quarry sites, bearing inscriptions or not, have been located along most of the central portion of the Wall: there are fewer at the east end, and possibly the Tyne was used to ship stone down from further afield for this sector. At the west end, where the turf wall was converted to stone, the lack of good building stone made the search for viable material more widespread still.

The facing stones of the wall were carefully cut and shaped, normally with a square or rectangular face allowing them to be set in neat courses. They were tail-bedded into a coursed core of stone set in stiff clay or capped with mortar, normally derived from much closer at hand than the quarries. Rebuilt portions of the wall later than the initial Hadrianic stages appear mainly to have been set in mortar, often of a hardness that renders it relatively impervious even to the weather, and at risk from damage only by the scrabbling of animals' or hikers' feet. Lime was burnt and slaked near

25 *The Roman temporary camps and other remains on Haltwhistle Common. Hadrian's Wall and Cawfields milecastle are visible at bottom right of the picture, near the water-filled Cawfields quarry, which has removed a portion of the wall's course. The vallum is clearly visible as a diagonal line across the bottom part of the picture, while beyond it are the traces of five temporary camps (B–F), as well as the site of Haltwhistle Burn fortlet (A) in a small enclosure perched above the burn. For a plan of this fortlet as excavated see* **14**.

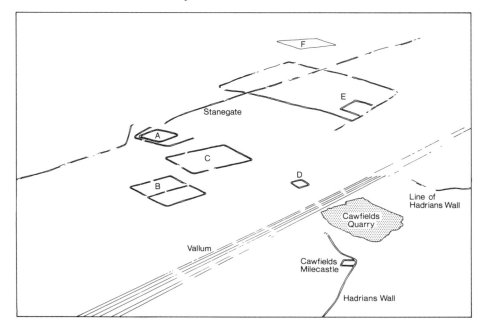

the wall, for limestone was readily available in the neighbourhood.

It remains to consider what the Wall actually looked like when built (26). Currently nowhere

26 *Sections across the Wall. These sketches show the probable original dimensions of the wall, as well as the height of the highest standing portion which has been excavated.*

does it survive to a height of more than 11 ft (3.3 m). Writing in the eighth century, the Venerable Bede, who lived at the monastery of Jarrow, described the wall as 8 ft wide and 12 ft high, though other, later, writers in the sixteenth century give different heights 'seven yards' (6.9 m), '16 foot' (5.2 m), or 'fifteen feet' (4.9 m). There is nothing inherently impossible, of course, in the view that the Wall was of different

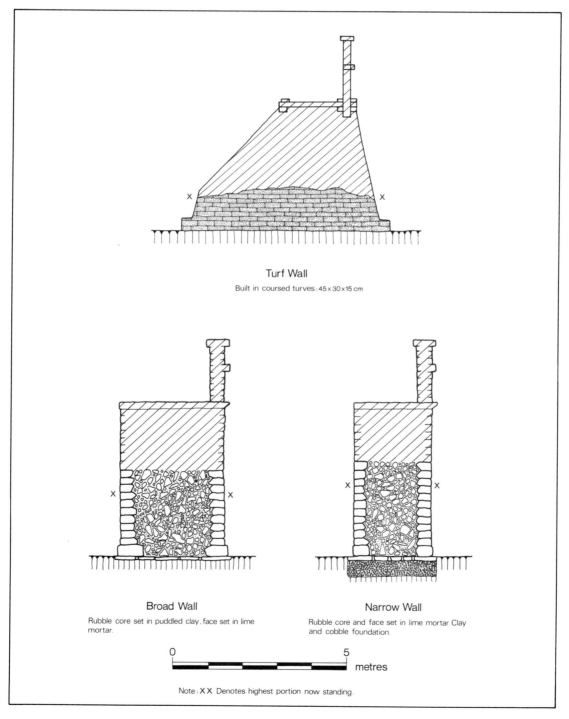

Turf Wall

Built in coursed turves: 45 x 30 x 15 cm

Broad Wall

Rubble core set in puddled clay, face set in lime mortar.

Narrow Wall

Rubble core and face set in lime mortar Clay and cobble foundation.

0   5

metres

Note: X X Denotes highest portion now standing.

heights at different places. We know, after all, that it was of different widths in different places, but there are other archaeological arguments which can be deployed.

The discovery at milecastle 48 of the base of a flight of steps within the north-east corner of the enclosure allows a calculation of the height these steps would have reached if they were continued at the angle they take at their foot before they were stopped by the outer milecastle wall. This produces a figure of no more than 15 ft (4.5 m) to their top. This, however, applies only to the milecastle walls, not necessarily to the wall-curtain itself: the two need not necessarily have been the same. In recent work at Willowford, however, which examined the area leading to the bridge, and the point of junction between the Broad and Narrow walls, the core of the Broad Wall built as part of the bridge was found to have been stepped down so that it all could remain stable until the rest of the Wall — in this case at a narrower gauge — could be brought up to it. The angle of the stepped-down broad wall core at this point, projected upwards to the end of the bridge structure suggests that the Wall can have been no less than $11\frac{1}{2}$ ft (3.5 m) and no more than 13 ft (about 4 m) high.

This calculation applies only to the body of the wall, not to any parapet or breastwork on its north side. That it probably was crenellated is shown by recent finds of stones which appear to have capped these embrasures within rubble which has tumbled from the north face of the wall. Pictorial representations of the wall — as on the Rudge cup (**27**) or a similar representation round a bronze bowl, the patera from Amiens — also seem to show a crenellated structure, but this could be a representation of the wall's turrets or milecastles rather than an attempt to show general crenellation running along the wall-top. It is often assumed that a platform existed at wall-walk level so that troops could patrol along the wall-top: it is however, far from certain that this was the case.

West of the River Irthing, where the Wall was built in turf, its height is generally thought to have been around 12 ft (3.6 m) though the only evidence for this is the width of the prepared base for the wall and the likely angle at which turves can be laid to form a long-lived barrier. This wall, however, had stone turrets which could have communicated at upper level with the top of the turf wall (**28**). It is not known whether the stone wall in this sector which replaced the turf one was of the same height: if it was not, there would have been problems over the incorporation of the turf wall turrets.

Evidence is also beginning to emerge that the Wall may have been rendered and whitewashed.

27 *The Rudge Cup, a small bronze bowl, decorated with inlaid enamel, found in 1725 within a well at a Roman villa site near Marlborough, Wiltshire. Its decoration shows a fortification consisting of a wall with regular crenellated towers, surmounted by an inscription which appears to list the names of the western group of Wall-forts, probably taken from a Roman road-book. It names Mais (Bowness), Aballava (Burgh by Sands), Uxelodum (Stanwix), Camboglans (Castlesteads) and Banna (Birdoswald).*

Excavations in the Castle Nick area have revealed elements of stonework which must have formed part of the facing stones of the wall — including a coping stone — which bear unmistakeable traces of whitewash. Closer to the east end of the Wall, at Denton, portions of the fallen facing stones of the wall have been revealed to have been rendered. The modern view of the Wall, therefore, with neat rows of cubed stone forming an instantly recognisable Roman facing, may be far from correct. We should perhaps be thinking in terms of a rendered face, scribed with false joints, and painted bright white: an impressive barrier indeed, though again this may not have applied to its full length.

Problems not only over the height of the Wall and its aspect, but also about how the wall turrets and milecastles originally looked have

exercised scholars for some time. It is generally agreed that the point of the turrets was to lift an observation post above the height of the normal wall, and it is likely that not only the turrets, but also the towers above the milecastle gateways through the Wall were intended to act in the same way. The stairs allowing access to the milecastle's north wall at Poltross Burn (milecastle 48) have already been mentioned: these suggest that there was a wall-walk — at least within the milecastle — and that access to any tower over the gateway would have been through an external door from the wall-walk

28 *Banks turret and the Turf Wall. This sketch shows the stone turret and the turf wall as originally built up to it. The height and the finish of the topmost part of the turret are conjectural.*

along the milecastle's north wall itself. No evidence, however, has been recovered from milecastles which would suggest whether towers above the gate were single or double storeyed, or whether they had a flat or a tiled and pitched roof.

Nor is there a great deal of evidence for completing the upper storeys of turrets (**colour plate 10**). Internally, turrets always appear to have a stone base, most sensibly interpreted as a platform for a ladder, allowing access to the upper floor or floors. Above wall-walk level (assuming that there was one), the turrets could have been raised one or two more storeys with ease: perhaps the most convincing suggestion about how they were completed is to look at the towers illustrated on Trajan's column in Rome which have formed the model for many life-sized reconstructed towers on the Roman German frontier today: here the top of the tower sports a wooden platform round all four sides allowing observation in all directions under cover of a pitched or gabled roof. Whilst it is perhaps too rigid a modern inference to draw to reconstruct all towers, precisely to the one design pictured on Trajan's column, this is nonetheless a satisfactory model and one at least which we know has the stamp of authenticity.

Hadrian's frontier thus progressed in its construction from east to west, and for about two years, it appears, until around the end of AD 124, all continued as planned: broad wall, with its clay and cobble foundations and core, its ditch, milecastles and turrets. The scheme was not very old, however, before changes began to be brought in.

4

The forts are added

As originally planned, the Wall was to have been built on higher ground north of the military road — the Stanegate. Apart from whatever space there might be in the milecastles, provision for accommodation of garrison troops who might man the Wall was left with the line of forts and fortlets from Corbridge to Carlisle which already lay along that road. At some point a fundamental change of plan took place, and forts were constructed along the line of the Wall itself (**29**). There are now known to be 16 forts either attached to the wall or in close association with it. It is probable that not all of these were built at the same time, but that the plan to locate them on the Wall line grew in stages. Archaeological evidence has been

able to piece together something of the sequence which must have been followed.

It is clear, first of all, that the provision of forts was only made after parts of the Broad Wall had been laid out and constructed. Some of the forts were planted in positions where they overlay the site of one of the Wall structures. In one instance, at Greatchesters, this is the site of a milecastle 43, while at other places — Chesters, Housesteads and Birdoswald — these are turrets 27a, 36b and 49a respectively. The evidence at Housesteads is particularly conclus-

29 *Map of Hadrian's Wall and its added forts, showing the developed form of the frontier by about AD 130.*

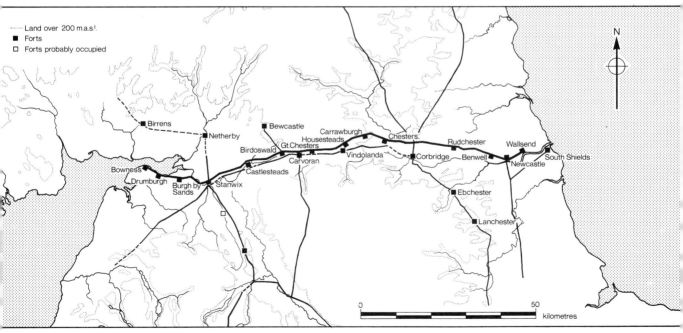

ive: here, in a site where the proximity of the sheer face of the Whin Sill to its north made the selection of the best ground for the north rampart of the fort a prime necessity, not only was turret 36b, already partially built, dismantled and levelled so that the fort could take its place, but the configuration of the course of Hadrian's Wall was altered at the points where it joined the newly built fort so that the fort's north wall could be pushed as far towards the edge of the scarp as it could go. At Chesters, too, excavators have shown that elements of the fort's defences had to be specially strengthened with deep foundations at the points where they crossed the site of the wall-ditch which had already been dug and which therefore formed less stable ground.

Not all forts, however, occupied the sites of turrets or milecastles. The best dating evidence for the construction of forts comes from Benwell and Haltonchesters, two of those which do not. From Benwell comes an inscription from the granaries proclaiming their construction by a detachment of workmen from the British fleet under the governor Aulus Platorius Nepos, the same man whose name appears on milecastle inscriptions, and another inscription with the same governor's name also came from one of the gates at Haltonchesters. Thus, within Nepos' governorship — that is, by 126 at the latest if his term as governor lasted the normal four or five years — the decision to build the forts had been taken, and work was sufficiently advanced for enough of them to have been completed and for their dedication stones to have been erected.

Despite their common purpose and contemporary construction, the new forts now added to the Wall are all slightly different, and there is no standard plan of their internal buildings. Certain common characteristics, however, are shared between them, for Roman forts throughout their empire had evolved to a similar if not an absolutely standard layout during the course of the first century AD. The temporary camp used by the army of the Roman Republic was described in the second century BC by the Greek writer Polybius, and it is clear that the installation he described already contained many of the elements of the fort-plan which we have come to regard as typically Roman. By the third century AD, when Hyginus described a standard pattern for a Roman fortress within his technical manual covering surveying techniques the layout was still substantially the same. Excavation has shown that, although there are sometimes surprising deviations from this overall design, by the time of Hadrian the planning and layout of a fort had reached something of a standard form with relatively minor variations.

In plan, the fort normally would look in outline like a playing card, rectangular with rounded corners, and approximately one and a half times as long as it is broad. The ramparts were normally of stone backed with earth though they could also be entirely of turf-and-timber, and were normally surrounded by at least one ditch with a V-profile in section. Midway along each of the short sides there would be a double-portalled entrance; the main gates in the two longer sides would be at opposite ends of a street running through the fort at about a third of the distance along it, leaving space for a subsidiary entrance, where this was needed, equidistant between this gate and the far end. The fort walls were backed on the inside by a rampart of earth which was interrupted by towers projecting inside the fort within the curve of the rounded corners and at intervals between them and the gates. This rampart area might on occasion be used for bakehouses, workshops and latrines, and was separated from the remainder of the buildings within the fort by a road which ran round the whole circuit.

The plan of the fort at Wallsend, virtually completely excavated between 1975 and 1984, is a good example of this internal layout (30). At the crossing point of the two main roads into the fort lay the entrance to the headquarters building (*principia*), which lay at the heart of the fort and straddled its central long axis. This occupied the central part of the middle third of the fort, while to its west lay other administrative buildings — a double granary with loading platforms to the south under a portico roof, and a workshop or hospital block. To its east was a relatively expansive house for the unit's Commanding Officer. This was of courtyard plan and although there was scant trace of this at Wallsend, at other places such houses contained their own underfloor heating systems and baths. The front and rear portions of the fort — its front faced the enemy with the majority of its gates issuing out forwards — were filled with accommodation for the troops in garrison and with other buildings which may have been stores, workshops or stables.

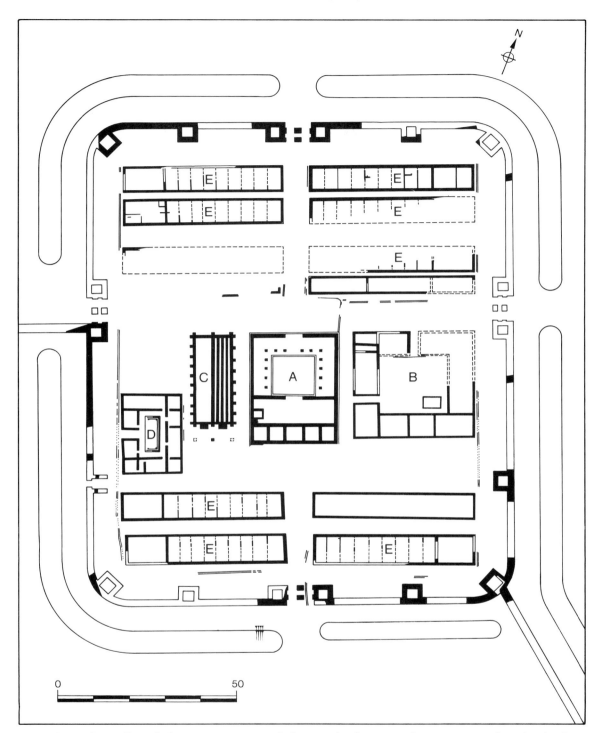

30 *Plan of Wallsend fort, as uncovered by excavations between 1977 and 1984. The Hadrianic plan of virtually the whole of the fort was examined in advance of proposals to use the site for housing and light industry. Although the site has now been preserved, only the layout of its walls and the headquarters building are now visible on the ground. On this plan (A) is the headquarters; (B) the commandant's house; (C) granaries; (D) hospital; and (E) a workshop.*

31 *Tombstone of an archer from Housesteads fort. This has been dated to the second century, but there is no other record of a unit of archers at Housesteads fort at that date: Carvoran, the next but one fort to the west, however, does appear to have had a garrison of archers in the Hadrianic period. Fragments of evidence like this have to be combined into an overall picture of which troops garrisoned the Wall forts.*

At Wallsend, in the earliest phases, remains of at least eight barrack blocks appear to have been located within the fort. These were all about 28 x 144 ft (8.5 x 44 m) long, with clay bonded outer walls resting on stone sills: those in the rear (southern) portion of the fort are typical of the kind of building familiar at many other forts. Of four narrow buildings, three appear to have been barracks. Approximately three-quarters of their length was subdivided by timber partitions into barrack rooms normally 9 in number, and this accommodated the men of a century, while the remaining portion, separated from the rest by a stone partition, was the quarters for their commanding officer, the centurion. The fourth building, although externally similar to the rest, had no traces of internal subdivision, and could have been a stable. Internal subdivisions of this type have enabled at least eight barracks to be identified out of twelve long buildings within the fort. What is most surprising, however, about the plan of Wallsend in its Hadrianic phase is the amount of space within the fort apparently left as open gravelled areas, and not occupied by buildings.

At no other fort has the original plan been recovered so completely as it has at Wallsend and at only two forts on the Wall — Housesteads and Chesters — can the remains of barrack blocks now be seen. The type of unit in garrison should be reflected in the size and number of the barrack blocks contained within each fort: if it was an auxiliary infantry cohort, for example, there would have been a paper strength of 480 men, divided into six *centuriae*, centuries of around 80 men each, thus requiring six barrack blocks. If it were a cavalry wing (*ala*), there would be 512 men, divided into 16 *turmae* (squadrons) of 32 men each, two of which might be accommodated within each barrack block, thus requiring eight such buildings.

However, the exercise of determining what sort of ground plan was actually required for particular units is fraught with difficulties (**31**). The picture is complicated by the existence within the Roman army of double strength (or nearly so) units, mixed units of cavalry and infantry, or of temporarily assembled special forces for particular tasks or campaigns. From our point of view, we need more detailed knowledge about the numbers of horses attached to individual units and therefore the sort of stabling accommodation they might require, or about what structural changes (some of them perhaps internal partitioning only within barrack blocks) were the norm when a fort was taken over by a new garrison of different type, before we can be certain what unit was in garrison from the plan of the accommodation within the fort.

1 The Wall-landscape under light snow-cover: Haltwhistle Common and
Cawfields, looking towards Housesteads. The modern road is the dark line to
the right of the picture, the Wall follows the crest of the crags towards its
centre. At the foot of the crags the line of the vallum can be seen striking in
the distance to converge with the road, and in the foreground are the traces of
several of the temporary camps to be seen in this area as well as Haltwhistle
Burn fortlet (see also **25**).

2 Impression of the way in which a hoard of armour and other materials found
in a wooden chest buried at Corbridge between AD 122 and 138 were
originally arranged in their box. The contents included portions of at least six
segmental cuirasses, spearheads, and ballista-bolts as well as a great variety
of tools, including a pulley-block and saw-blades.

3 Model of a Roman soldier wearing a replica of one of the suits of armour discovered in the hoard at Corbridge. Although these cuirasses are normally associated with legionary soldiers, they are increasingly being found at sites where auxiliary cavalry were based.

4 The Corbridge lion, originally a
tomb-monument, was found
during excavations of a large
building on the terrace above the
River Tyne in 1907. It had been
re-used as a fountain within a
cistern. The lion triumphantly
holds the stag down with his
paws, while his victim seems
limply to accept its fate.

5 Part of the frieze from a temple of
Jupiter Dolichenus at Corbridge,
carved in two-dimensional relief.
The scene shows Sol (the sun-
god) riding in on his winged
horse from the left towards an
open colonnaded building within
which stands one of the Dioscuri
(Castor or Pollux). To the right
hand edge of the stone are a tree
and the figure of a youth, possibly
Apollo. The missing portion of
the stone would probably have
shown the other Dioscurus and
the goddess Luna; all five of
these figures make up a common
combination of Apollo and
his attendants.

6 Impression of the bridge rebuilt in the early third century to carry Hadrian's Wall across the River Tyne at Chesters. Elements of the carved stonework shown in this reconstruction can still be seen lying on or near the site of the eastern abutment (see also **23-4**).

7 The Hadrianic bridge at Willowford, according to recent interpretation and survey, was of stone. It crossed the river on a number of low arches, and sprang from the stone wall on the eastern side, where traces of its abutment are still visible. This reconstruction view shows the turf wall commencing at the west end of the bridge, for from about this point westwards, Hadrian's Wall was originally built in turf rather than stone.

10 Brunton turret (no 26b) as it may originally have appeared when first built. The arrangements of the turrets above wall-walk level are conjectural, but are based on carved representations of towers on Trajan's column set up in the early second century in Rome.

top left

8 The courtyard of the headquarters building at Chesters. The open courtyard was surrounded by a verandah and afforded access to the large high hall which lay across the further end of the building.

bottom left

9 The east gate of Chesters fort from the outside. The gate opens out to the north of the Wall, and part of the Wall-ditch has had to be backfilled to allow access to it.

11 Hadrian's Wall near Cawfields.

Questions about which garrison was responsible for the original Hadrianic construction of any given fort are therefore not easily answered. In many cases, although we do know the unit in occupation at various times (from inscriptions recording building, for example), the original garrison is often unknown, and a guess can only be made as to the type of unit which occupied the fort from its original plan or size. In the Hadrianic army, units were relatively mobile, and a measure of permanence in the frontier zone was only achieved in the third century, when, as far as we can see, many of the Wall garrisons took up positions which they were to hold for nearly 150 years. The amount of accommodation for the Hadrianic garrison at Wallsend, for example, leads to the conclusion that it was originally intended for a part-mounted cohort of around 500 men: excavation has shown, however, that the barrack accommodation was altered on more than one occasion, and inscriptions show that both an infantry cohort (the *cohors II Nerviorum*) and a part-mounted cohort (the *cohors IV Lingonum*) later occupied the fort at different times.

For good examples of the plan or layout of other elements of forts it is necessary to look at surviving remains at various places along the Wall's line. Fort defences and gates can be seen at Chesters (**32**), Greatchesters, Housesteads and Birdoswald (**33**) in particular. Elsewhere, although nothing other than earthworks may now be visible, the grassy mounds of the distinctive ramparts of other forts are easily identifiable features. Birdoswald, where the fort walls still front a considerable build-up of apparently undisturbed rampart, has perhaps the best surviving example of walls and fort gates.

The main fort gates were double-portalled, admitting two carriageways for wheeled traffic separated by a central spine. In both forts and milecastles, gateways were built of more massive stone than the remainder of their walls: their jambs and semicircular arches were built of large stone, carefully cut and shaped. At Chesters, the threshold stones and the large socket-holes with iron collars in which the gate pivots themselves turned can still be seen, and there are central stop-blocks to stop the gates

32 *The east gate at Chesters, looking through the double portal from outside the fort. Compare the reconstruction drawing,* **colour plate 9.**

33 *View of the east gate at Birdoswald undergoing consolidation and clearance. The north portal of the dual-carriageway gate is clearly visible. The stop-block for the leaves of the gate and the large stone of the gate-jambs, including one stone of the arch itself, are all in position.*

swinging open too far. Gates were normally flanked by a pair of guard-chambers, opening out either onto the fort or into the gate's entrance passage. Many of the fort gateways were walled up after the Hadrianic period, suggesting that the provision of so many double passageways was not really necessary: at others, the wear and tear was so heavy that they were re-floored several times. At Chesters and Birdoswald, elements of the gates survive still standing to the point where the archway begins, but the design of the gate above that point is more conjectural (**colour plate 9; 97**, p.131). It is likely that they carried an inscription commemorating the construction-work and there is likely to have been a chamber at wall-walk level above the gate-passages and at upper levels in the flanking towers. These would be lit by narrow round-headed windows. The form of the roof is a problem: excavation at some gates has produced evidence for stone slates or roofing tiles, but some of them may equally well have had flat roofs with a further observation platform.

A number of buildings often occupied the fort's rampart area. Subsidiary gates and interval towers, the rain from their roofs often supplying water-tanks nearby, studded the walls themselves, and bake-houses and ovens, carefully separated from the other buildings in the fort because of the fire-risk, occupied the rampart areas. Such ovens can be seen at the west gate of Chesters, and by the south gate at Birdoswald, while bakehouses belonging to the earliest phase of the fort at Housesteads have been located by excavation. At Housesteads, too, can be seen a good example of a fort latrine which lay at the lowest point on the fort so that it could be kept supplied with water to flush it (**34**). Wooden seats, long since disappeared, were suspended above a channel which could be easily flushed and allow the effluent to be deposited in the fort ditch just beyond the wall. A latrine at Vindolanda is tucked in a similar position in the corner of the fort.

The most important of the internal buildings was the headquarters — the *principia*. The best example can be seen at Chesters, where, as in most of the other forts, it lay at the end of the street which led straight into the fort from the main north gate (**35, colour plate 8**). Its main door gives on to a large open courtyard still partially paved with large stone slabs: this incorporates an opening for a well with nearby a carving of a good luck phallus clearly picked out on one of the stones. Round three sides of this courtyard there was an open colonnade where orders could be posted.

From the courtyard and from each of the colonnades, double doors led into a large hall set across the line of the building. This was used for meetings, hearings, briefing sessions and ceremonial occasions. At one end was a platform, the *tribunal,* where the commanding officer would take his place: elsewhere there were traces of bases for statues and altars. The headquarters was the seat of discipline, duty, morale, and loyalty, a place sacred to the garrison.

Off its north side lay a range of smaller rooms most of which were used as offices for clerks. The central one, barred off from the rest of the building by a stone screen somewhat like an altar-rail, was the regimental chapel (**36**). Here,

34 *The latrine at the south-east corner of the fort at Housesteads. A system of water-tanks, one of which is visible beyond and to the left of the latrine, stored water used to flush the channels. The paved central island was the entry to the wooden latrines suspended over the channel for effluent.*

35 *View across the courtyard of the head-quarters building, Chesters. Compare the similar view reconstructed in* **colour plate 8**.

statues of the reigning emperor were kept, and, doubtless, the regimental standards too. As well as a focus for loyalty, the chapel often acted as a safe for regimental pay and several head-quarters buildings contain or give access to underground strong rooms.

The commandant's house, next to the head-quarters, was a remarkably luxurious and expansive residence for the unit's commanding officer, his family and personal staff. At Chesters there is a highly complex set of remains of such a house, with many later additions and improvements, but the simpler original form survives in the building at Housesteads (**37**). Here on a far from level site the house is arranged round four sides of a courtyard. It incorporates kitchens, latrines, and stabling as well as domestic accommodation, some of it provided with underfloor heating. Parts of the house may have been two-storeyed, and this will

have afforded a substantial amount of working and living space for the commandant, his staff and servants. The courtyard building, which has similarities with Roman town houses else-where in Britain as well as in Italy, is more than just a concession to luxury: it is more a sign of the elevated social status of the unit commander: one of the routes upwards to a full political career was through commands in the army, and men posted even to the northern British frontier might be rising politically, socially and financially.

Housesteads, too, provides good examples of the other official buildings in the fort's central area. One is the hospital (**38**). This, too, is arranged round a central courtyard though smaller in scale than the commandant's house, with a series of rooms — possibly wards — leading off it, and, in one corner, a latrine. There is actually nothing in the plan and design of this building to show what it was used for: nor were any of the finds associated with it conclusively indicative that it was a hospital. Similar buildings elsewhere have been claimed

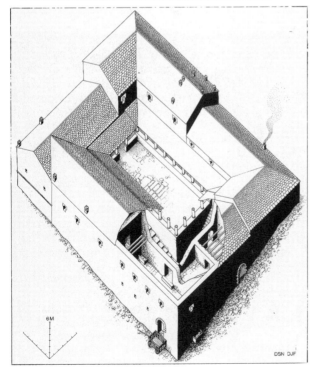

36 *The entrance to the 'regimental chapel' in the headquarters building at Vindolanda. The stone threshold, with grooves for upright stones, one of which is in its original position, can be clearly seen.*

37 *Sketch of the commandant's house at Housesteads. This large and complex courtyard house was built on a site which sloped severely; this drawing attempts to show how it may have looked, with all the changes in level required for its siting.*

38 *Artist's impression of the interior courtyard of the hospital building at Housesteads. As with all fort buildings, it is uncertain whether they were of stone for the whole of their height: here it is suggested that upper storeys may have been half-timbered.*

to be workshops on the basis of the traces of industrial processes discovered within them. There is nothing inherently improbable, however, in a standard plan of a courtyard building being pressed into service for any one of a number of functions — whether as workshop, hospital, administrative offices, armoury, or even, if need arose, for extra domestic accommodation.

The final building in the central area is the stores (**39**). Often described as the 'granaries', this name is something of a misnomer, for the store-buildings were probably used for all kinds of foodstuffs as well as grain, and possibly for other supplies too. The best example of a building of this type, though it is archaeolog-

ically complex, is to be seen at Housesteads, and there are also fine surviving buildings of the same form at Corbridge and excavation is in the process of uncovering others at Birdoswald (see **83**, p. 114). All of these, however, are of later date than the Hadrianic period: those at Birdoswald, for example, were probably the store-buildings whose rebuilding was recorded on an inscription dated AD 205–6 found at the fort.

The original Hadrianic store-building at Housesteads was a large, double-storeyed building, with double loading doors at its west end, so as to be well away from the entrance to the headquarters. Its upper floor was supported by a row of columns or pillar bases which stretched along its length, and the ground floor was supported on smaller pillars to keep perishables well ventilated and as free from vermin as possible. Buttresses along the sides gave the building lateral strength, as well as providing for archaeologists of today a distinctive plan and the basis for endless arguments about what

the superstructure looked like. Many store buildings were narrow, often four times longer than they were wide. Those at Corbridge always formed two separate structures, and each was buttressed on both sides: the Housesteads building, originally a single large storehouse, was later subdivided into two more normal-sized

39 *View of the north granary at Housesteads. The pillars supported a suspended floor, and the external wall (to left) was buttressed on the outside. The Housesteads granary was at first a single larger store-building, and the walls to the right were inserted later to divide the building into two.*

40 *The vallum at Limestone corner, looking west. The ditch is cut through solid rock; a pile of rocks extracted from it lie to the right on the north mound. South of the ditch are two mounds: the south mound of the vallum is the further one, and it has been later cut through at intervals when the vallum was slighted later in the second century. The mound nearest the ditch seems to have been the result of scouring the ditch.*

ones. The Birdoswald granaries seem only to have been buttressed on their southern side, perhaps to compensate for sloping ground within the fort.

Wallsend fort was built at the same time as the portion of Hadrian's Wall which strikes about 4 miles (6½ km) eastwards from the site of the river-crossing at Newcastle. This stretch of wall was an afterthought, a later extension to the curtain, possibly built at the same time as the addition of forts to the rest of the Wall. Like Benwell and Halton, Wallsend straddles the wall-line, with its northern third, including three of its main double portalled gateways, projecting beyond it, a pattern followed by several others, including Chesters, Rudchester and Birdoswald, which straddles the turf wall in the same way that other forts straddle the stone wall. This common relationship to the wall seems to be a sign that these forts were

among the first to be added to the wall. Some of the other forts which do not follow the same plan, like Bowness or Housesteads, may also have belonged to this early series. At these sites the lie of the ground made it impracticable for a third of the fort's area to project to the north of the Wall.

An emerging pattern is that about a dozen of the Wall forts were built on the Wall line as a first stage, spaced at about 7½ Roman miles (11 km) apart, and some of them sited at strategic points — Chesters, for example, at the crossing of the River Tyne, Birdoswald near the crossing of the River Irthing, and Stanwix, the biggest and the strongest of the forts on the Wall's line, at the crossing of the River Eden. Much of the precise detail of the foundation dates of individual forts, however, still needs to be determined. At present it appears that all sixteen forts closely associated with the Wall were built by the end of Hadrian's reign.

Only at this stage, when forts were under construction, was the decision taken to add a further element to the defensive scheme. This was to dig at some distance south of the Wall the earthwork known today as the 'vallum', which is a broad flat-bottomed ditch flanked by a pair of linear banks (**40**). This shadows the wall for almost all of its course, though it has not been traced between central Newcastle and

Wallsend (**41**). Visible today for considerable portions of the Wall's length, the vallum, probably known to the Romans as '*fossatum*', defines a course sometimes very close to the Wall, and sometimes as much as a kilometre to its south. That it was added after the decision to place forts on the Wall is shown by the fact that its course deviates in places to avoid wall-forts. In one or two places where the relationship has up to now been examined, a causeway was left in the vallum ditch so that any main trackway leading to the south gate of the forts would not be interrupted. At Benwell, there was a crossing point for the vallum ditch as it runs up to the south gate of the fort: the causeway was controlled from the fort-side by a large gateway which entirely blocked the carriageway (**42**). Remains of a similar causeway have also been traced at Birdoswald, where the tight fit of the fort onto the level ground above the Irthing gorge made it difficult to

41 *The vallum ditch, emptied of its fill, during the excavations undertaken in 1987 on the line of the Newcastle western ring-road. The ditch was of substantial depth and flat-bottomed.*

complete the vallum's north mound.

The vallum has excited a great deal of speculation as to its purpose, and this will be more properly dealt with in the next chapter, but one of its subsidiary purposes, it seems, was to link the forts on the wall with a method of lateral communication. When forts were placed on the wall-line, no provision appears to have been made for a road to link them: the only provision was for communication southwards back onto the Stanegate which was to be the main east–west route. It was clearly found rather impracticable to retain this idea, and therefore, a metalled track was provided in places along the vallum between north mound and ditch

42 *Impression of the gate which guarded the vallum crossing due south of Benwell fort. It was placed on the fort side of the causeway over the vallum ditch, and the gates were worked from the fort side of the crossing.*

along which lateral communication could be made more easily.

The close interrelationship between all these elements of the wall system — the wall and its structures, the forts and the vallum — is compounded by the discovery that at least one fort, Carrawburgh, actually lies over the filled in vallum ditch. Carrawburgh, its construction usually dated to the Hadrianic period from an inscription of the fourth cohort of Aquitanians apparently at the fort in AD 130–3, does not

project north of Hadrian's Wall, but seems rather to have been added to the Wall after the fashion of a large milecastle. Its walls butt up against the Narrow Wall, and the indications are that it was yet another afterthought.

Other forts may also have been afterthoughts: Greatchesters, although its spacing suggests that it could have been one of the primary forts, sits on the site of a milecastle, and has a similar relationship to the narrow Wall: here, however, no clues are given by its relationship with the vallum for this is some distance to the south. Too little is known of others to give an accurate definition of where they fit within the system though both Newcastle at the east end and Drumburgh at the west may have been further additions to the original scheme.

The sequence of events at the western end of the Wall is less easy to define. From Willowford bridge westwards the wall was built of turf rather than stone; when Birdoswald fort was added to the wall — possibly itself originally in turf and timber — it straddled the turf wall, including the site of the turf wall turret 49a. At a later stage the whole of the turf wall was removed and replaced in stone on the same line, except for a short stretch round Birdoswald fort. Examination of finds from the turf wall milecastle no 50, which was never built over by the stone wall, suggests that its occupation did not outlast Hadrian's reign, and there is evidence for only a single phase of use. Moreover, evidence from turrets along the stretch of replacement stone wall not on the line of the earlier turf structures (between Birdoswald and turret 51a) has suggested that pottery and other material here dates from the Hadrianic phase. It is, however, very difficult to assign an accurate date to small assemblages of material from contexts such as these to within about 30–40 years. It may yet be discovered that the stone wall in the Birdoswald area was built in the 160s rather than during Hadrian's reign.

—— 5 ——
What was the Wall for?

Hadrian's Wall was built by troops, and was thus the product of strategic planning, whether locally in Britain or in Rome. The fact that it seems to have been begun immediately after Hadrian's visit to Britain suggests that it was in some measure at least the personal initiative of the emperor. During his tour round western European provinces, Hadrian was concerned to boost army morale, improve its discipline and standards of living, and to set it on a sound professional footing (see p. 29). The construction of the Wall in Britain, as well as the consolidation also carried out at almost the same time on the frontier in Germany, has to be seen in this context, as well as reflecting the mood of realism which followed in the wake of the 'golden age' of Trajan.

It is important to examine the strategic and tactical considerations surrounding the construction of the Wall as they built up, and as extra components were added to the scheme. It may not make sense, for example, to examine the decision to place forts on the wall unless the altering shift of planning that this entailed can be grasped. To understand it fully, some consideration of what the wall scheme without forts was at first seeking to achieve will be necessary. Similarly, some assessment of the underlying motives and the shifts in Roman policy which the wall's construction reveals has to be attempted. It is not enough to be amazed at the industry and energy of the legionaries who built the wall under their emperor's orders. Government expenditure of that nature and that order normally reflects an attempt to fulfil a perceived need, even if, when viewed with the benefit of hindsight, this can be seen to be misguided one.

The Wall was a barrier, to be sure. But what was it for? Did it keep people in, or out? Was it a defended line or did it stake out territory? As planned from the beginning, its presence was a substantial bar to anyone whose business, authorised or illicit, took them on north–south routes into southern Scotland. The barrier was not, however, total. There was provision for a gateway in every mile of its length, within a series of suitably protected, but rather chill and sunless, and therefore inhospitable, small enclosures, the milecastles. These were not all placed so as to encourage traffic or passage through the wall: at Sewingshields for example, no north gate has been found, and at Cawfields the milecastle seems almost perversely to avoid a narrow gap which might have allowed easier access through the wall. There is something mechanical about their regular spacing which suggests that their provision may not have originally been carefully considered. There cannot have been as many pre-existing routes from north to south as there are milecastles, and this planning of gateways, as well as the execution of the scheme by the military builders, was automatic and standardised to cope with all possible eventualities for access in both directions through the Wall.

At the most conservative estimate, the stone wall and the turf wall were at least 13 ft (4 m) high. This is not an insuperable barrier to someone determined to cross it, but it certainly is a hindrance to rapid progress by considerable numbers of men, and to the passage of livestock or wheeled vehicles. Its presence, therefore, could cause considerable inconvenience to a local people who relied on the transhumance of flocks and herds between lowland feeding grounds in winter and those of the upland in summer. It would also effectively prevent raiders from the north from plundering live-stock or substantial amounts of foodstuffs from south of the wall and carrying it home unchallenged. It would act as a control on goods brought south from lowland Scotland for market, or on those exported northwards for the same purpose. If customs dues were to be levied by border guards, this is precisely the sort of comprehensive barrier which would be required to ensure that it was made extremely difficult to avoid payment.

The Wall seems to have been built in Brigantian territory, a tribe whose history would not have inspired Roman confidence that they, like other Celtic tribes in the south, would ever happily settle into a style of life which accepted Roman conventions and administrative systems, and become an effectively civilised unit. Indeed, it is not certain whether the Brigantes had a visible nucleus, a tribal heartland, at all. Even into the second century AD, their settlement sites, small nucleated farmsteads, show no overt sign of any Roman influence, apart from a scatter of luxury goods which could be interpreted as the product either of trade or brigandage. There is little evidence that a tribal elite of noblemen, who could accept the Roman political and social forms with readiness and thus school the rest of their followers in the same way, could be found to exist. The Roman tribal 'capital' of this area, *Isurium Brigantium*, at Aldborough, appears never to have been a large or successful town: it contains a scatter of buildings with mosaics, and traces of public buildings, but it was not large and, even when it was later walled, it enclosed only a restricted area, within which there seem always to have been substantial portions without buildings. Local enthusiasm for romanisation, or perhaps the lack of a local hegemony which could lead the way into the brave new Roman existence, may therefore have been lacking. The Romans clearly had a problem converting of such people to the benefits they offered: the Brigantes' inclination may have been to remain persistently barbarian.

While the Roman army was still engaged in hopes and dreams of conquest in Scotland, seeking to include the whole of lowland Scotland within the bounds of their 'civilised' world, the problems posed by tribes such as the Brigantes perhaps figured less immediately in the strategic considerations of Roman army planners. Once the concentration of Roman forces

had settled in force along the isthmus between Tyne and Solway, on the Stanegate line, however, the Brigantes posed a more pressing difficulty. We do not know precisely how far north Brigantian territory stretched: quite possibly there were strong links between tribes in parts of southern Scotland and those of northern England. With Roman withdrawal from Scotland, perhaps under pressure from these same tribesmen as well as for the Romans' own tactical reasons, contact between the Brigantes and their northern neighbours may well have become a considerable destabilising influence.

In this light, the statement by Hadrian's biographer that the Wall was to 'separate Romans from barbarians' gains added weight. The Wall was to mark the reasonable limit of spread of *Romanitas* — the process of absorption of native style, culture and lifestyle and adapting them into the Roman system of administration and social class which was the hallmark of the Roman presence in much of the western empire. The fact that the town of Aldborough was founded in the Hadrianic period suggests that it and the Wall, the one to provide the positive Roman focus, the other to concentrate the minds and contacts of those within the Roman world inwards rather than outwards, were part of the same plan. Thus the Wall can be seen as much as a barrier to keep people in as to keep unwholesome influences out. But, as we have already seen, it was a means of control, a potential source of revenue, as well as a sheer physical barrier.

If Hadrian's Wall, therefore, is to be seen as the equivalent of the modern-day wire fence and cleared strip, with carefully controlled crossing points, the provision of border guards, customs posts and garrisons was clearly of paramount importance. In the initial scheme, only milecastles and turrets lay on the Wall's line. Forts, permanent bases for men, lay on the Stanegate road, a short distance to the south. It is not altogether clear what provision there was originally for accommodation for men within the milecastles: only at milecastle 39, where only half the internal area still bore traces of the earliest phases, and at Sewingshields, where the earliest building encountered was a small one, taking up only a quarter or so of the available internal space, has modern excavation provided any sort of answer to the question (see fig **81**, p. 107). At milecastle 39, the earliest phases were

of timber and may well have been buildings occupying the two sides of the internal area — sufficient space perhaps for a half a *centuria*, or no more than 40 men, and very probably less. The turrets, if they provided accommodation for men at all, can hardly have held many more than 12 men, though much of this calculation depends upon how many storeys they had. In any case there can have been no more than 60 men at the outside, to each Wall mile. What is more, these troops would have been in very cramped and not at all pleasant conditions. If men in such numbers were to be stationed on the Wall full-time, a permanent full garrison of around 5,000 men, or the equivalent of ten auxiliary units, would be required to be housed in its structures.

It is clear that watching and patrolling was

43 *Peel gap tower, added to Hadrian's Wall soon after its construction to form a third 'turret' in wall-mile 39–40. In many respects similar to a turret, this tower had a platform (for a stair to the upper storeys?) outside its west wall — beyond the tower's remains in this picture — rather than within it.*

one of the primary functions on the barrier from the first. Milecastle gateways as well as turrets bore towers with good views to north as well as to south, back to the Stanegate. Signal towers which had been built before the wall were also incorporated into its line. Even so, some of its structures were sited very strangely. One tower, recently found, lay at the foot of Peel Gap (**43**). Although it differs in detail

61

from some of the turrets, and is actually the third 'turret' in this particularly long gap between milecastles, it is hardly sited to best advantage for views along the Wall. Its sight-line eastwards is cut off immediately by the crags. Whether signals could be telegraphed or sent by smoke codes from one end of the Wall to the other is not known, but turrets and milecastles were close enough to be easily intervisible. The reason for this extra 'turret' at Peel Gap is not immediately apparent, except perhaps to show that the planners of the Wall felt some unease about a long gap without a watchtower, and eventually made extra provision for it. A far better prospect from the tower, however, would have been gained some 330 ft (100 m) to its east, on the summit of Peel Crag.

Further clues about the Wall's function come from the stretch of wall in the flatter ground of the Solway Firth (44). This stretch of mudflats and shallow water was evidently fordable in several places, and the Wall was therefore continued as a full barrier up to the point at Bowness beyond which no further fords existed. Its purpose, quite clearly, was to control access and to ensure that no unauthorised arrivals, in force or otherwise, appeared on the Cumbrian coast. Yet even beyond Bowness, the state of watchfulness was maintained by a series of milefortlets and towers spaced, like the wall milecastles and turrets, at intervals of one mile (1.6 km) and of a third of a mile (536 m) and respectively (which ran for a further 26 miles (41 km) down the coast. Like the milecastles along the turf wall, these milefortlets were built of turf and timber, and they contained wooden buildings (45). One or two are indeed larger than the exiguous milecastles and count almost as small fortlets, but one, at Biglands, just west of Bowness fort, which has been excavated, was certainly occupied in the Hadrianic and at several later stages too. Unlike the milecastles on the nearby Wall, however, these small fortlets were never converted to stone, though the towers between them, like the turf wall turrets, were built in stone from the first.

Precise details of the sequence of structures in this area are still lacking: research is beginning to show that the succession of defensive arrangements here may have been as complex as that of the Wall itself and that it will require a good deal of unravelling. A timber palisade seems at some stage to have been linked with this system as well as a single or double ditch

often of no great size. Near tower 4b, a ditch and a palisade or fence of timber, itself renewed, was found, together with traces of a clay base, which the excavators have suggested was the foundations for a timber tower predating the stone one. The slight nature of both ditch and palisade, however, is in marked contrast to the massive palisades discovered on the German frontier in association with timber towers.

The system of towers and small forts along the Cumbrian coast must have been to continue the control of shipping across the estuary of the Solway Firth, and to reinforce the authorised crossing points provided on the line of the turf wall between Bowness and the crossing of the River Eden at Carlisle. By the time that this coastal system was laid out, however, the forts at Kirkbride and at Maryport already existed: part at least of the system of towers and milefortlets seems to have been measured out working northwards from Maryport fort, and could have been a later development which took place after the decision to mount the forts themselves on Hadrian's barrier.

It has in the past been suggested that the Wall was not so much a method of control of traffic, but a defensible barrier or fighting platform on which Roman troops could stand to repel barbarian invasions. As has already been observed, if it was only a matter of 13 ft (4 m) or so high, the Wall could be relatively easily scaled, and even the presence of a ditch at its base would not make it an impossible obstacle to a determined band of men under cover of darkness. There is no evidence, however, that barbarian 'troops' ever actually stormed the Wall — not that archaological evidence would necessarily show this in any case — nor are there records of damage to buildings by enemy action. The picture of scaling ladders and defensive alarms, with Roman troops responding to a sizeable attack on the barrier is probably fiction.

First, the numbers of men who may have been deployed along the Wall as part of its original plan would make it virtually impossible for its immediate defenders to answer a sizeable attack in force. Second, there is no unequivocal evidence for a fighting platform on the wall top in any case: the Wall was, after all, not like a city defence which had a perimeter easily reached by the defending force, and which could be used in times of siege to pelt the attackers with missiles. It was a long barrier, the Roman

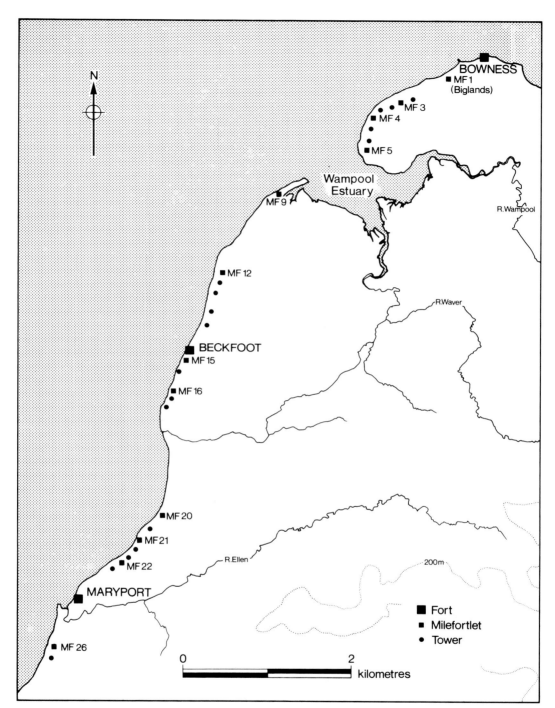

44 *Milefortlets and towers on the Cumbrian coast. The series of milefortlets and towers, similar in many respects to the milecastles and turrets of the turf wall, continues beyond Bowness to the Wampool estuary, and includes the larger fortlet of Cardurnock. South of the Wampool, elements of the spacing indicate that the system was laid out similarly, but working northwards from the fort at Maryport. The modern numbering allows for a number of lost sites around the estuary, but these may never in fact have existed.*

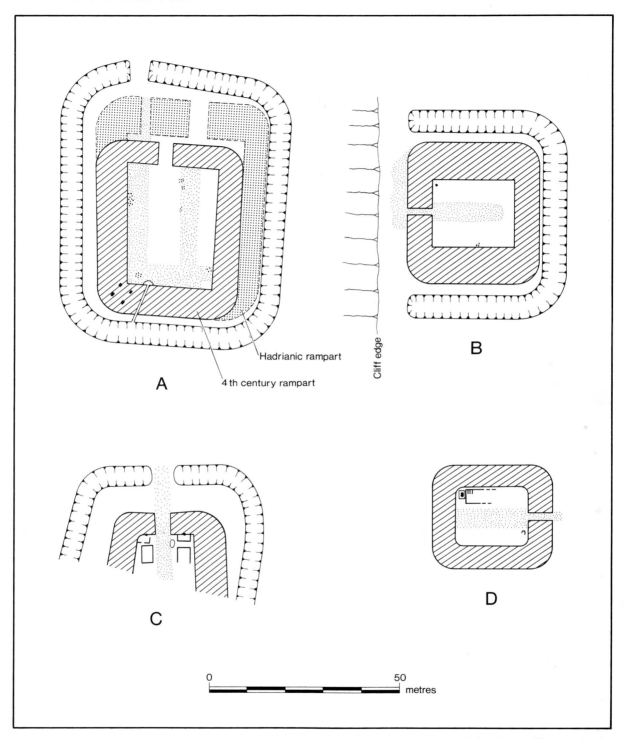

Cliff edge

Hadrianic rampart

4th century rampart

A

B

C

D

0   50
                        metres

45 *Comparative plans of milefortlets: (A) milefortlet 5 (Cardurnock); (B) milefortlet 22 (Brownrigg); (C) milefortlet 1 (Biglands), Hadrianic period; (D) milefortlet 20 (Low Mire).*

equivalent of heavy gauge wire netting and barbed wire, intended to hamper access, not to contest it *in situ*. There may indeed have been a wall walk, but it cannot have been part of the firm original planning to have sufficient men ready at all times to answer the rare call to contest an attempt at crossing. Bands of serious marauders who crossed the Wall would be mopped up by regular patrols in the hinterland. The presence of the wall behind them made their means of retreat more difficult, and this must have acted as sufficient disincentive to any direct military attack on the wall.

Conversely, the Wall has also been seen as a potential launch-pad for answering such a potential threat by allowing Roman troops to issue through the numerous gates, and pin a determined enemy against its face with a pincer movement. It must be remembered that in the Hadrianic scheme, where there were gates at every mile, the number of troops, even in a 4- or 5-mile (6–8 km) section of wall, was limited to 300 at the most. Even by calling up reinforcements from the nearest Stanegate fort, which might be 6–7 miles (9–11 km) away, the prospect of rapid deployment of troops in this way would have been remote, and the response time relatively slow. Nor is it certain that issuing through available milecastle gateways and turning to pin attackers against the barrier is necessarily the best tactical policy. To pin an enemy down with no hope of retreat may make resistence more desperate, and the whole tenor of the wall barrier is one of control and surveillance, not of hunting down the enemy and killing him. Dispersal of threats to the Wall would be better than cooping them up in one place, and a show of force without the need to come to blows might better serve the needs of the occasion. In any case, the Vindolanda tablets tell us that the 'wretched Britons do not stop and fight', preferring a mobile attack from horseback and evidently guerrilla tactics rather than a full-scale confrontation. The use of the Wall either as a fighting platform or as a tactical shield was probably not in the Roman planners' minds.

But what was Hadrian's intention? Apart from these practical considerations — those of border control, of separation of the Brigantes from their disruptive neighbours, of a measure of preclusive security — what other motives were there? For if the Wall was built actually to mark the limit of Rome's empire, to signify

the extent to which Rome could hope to control the peoples under its sway, then this is a momentous event indeed. Up until this point, Roman armies had been specialists in expansion, and had excelled at taking the fight to the enemy. There had been setbacks, to be sure — the defeat of three legions in Germany in AD 9, an event from which Augustus never recovered, or the gradual withdrawal (for whatever reason) of troops from Scotland between AD 90–105 — but the general exercise of the army's powers had been to suggest that its potential was unlimited. Trajan's campaigns, deep into the heart of Persia, had shown how all-pervasive was the might of Rome: but had he stretched too far?

Is Hadrian's Wall, therefore, the first sign of a realisation in the imperial councils that Rome's power was limited? Far from being a great and grandiose achievement, is it a sign of defeat, of incipient entrenchment, a reversal of the aggressive mentality into one which was defensive and watchful?

This attitude was later to manifest itself in the construction of massive walls round forts and towns, including Rome itself. But if acceptance of Rome's limitations was the theme which underlies the construction of Hadrian's wall, the chosen mode of displaying the fact is in itself an impressive one. The construction of a massive barrier running 80 miles (117 km) from sea to sea to separate Roman from barbarian is hardly an overt sign of absolute defeat. There are signs that towards its eastern end between Wallsend and Tynemouth, there was an additional triumphal monument to commemorate the conquest of Britannia. This was the natural foil to the massive entrance arch to the province erected by the emperor Domitian at Richborough, and marked out Rome's territory in typically uncompromising fashion. The Wall itself, studded with towers, possibly bristling with crenellations, strode purposefully from height to height. Gleaming new, with fresh pointing and possibly even rendered and whitewashed, this was intended to impress its presence upon those permitted to cross it, and even more so on those who were considered undesirable and thus excluded.

Quite apart from this, however, are the questions of what Hadrian may have been trying to achieve for his troops. He knew of the hardships of camp life, and possibly recognised the problems of men left exposed to the stress of chance

46 *The stone east abutment of Willowford bridge. This has been left some distance away from the river by the movement of the Irthing as it sweeps around the bend below the fort of Birdoswald and milecastle 49. These remains, most of which belong to the bridge built in the early third century to carry the military road across the river, are part of one of the piers and a flood relief channel, with the line of Hadrian's Wall as it approaches the river in the background.*

attack, or of frontier duty on an extensible frontier zone. He lived with his troops, talked to them, and perhaps more than any other emperor, strove to communicate with them and understand life at their level. His biographer relates how, when on his travels in the Gallic, German (and possibly British) provinces, he put on an old cloak and mixed in with the men in their mess rooms or round the camp fires. The Wall — his Wall — may therefore have given them a sense of added security, a feeling of superiority and the edge over the chance attack. It provided a marked disincentive to

attack and thus vastly improved the conditions of the garrison soldiers. Another consideration, by no means a minor one, was that the construction of such a large undertaking would absorb valuable man-hours possibly otherwise spent in watching and waiting, in duties like cleaning out the baths or the latrines. Those who had helped build Hadrian's great frontier would find a cause equal to their own expectations of Rome's grandeur and would also be loyal to the emperor who had conceived it. It was a task in which all could become involved, and, incidentally, it would keep idle hands busy.

The whole thrust of Hadrian's frontier policy was to define those inside the empire. This would enable those inside to feel they belonged to a social and economic framework which was increasingly able to spread its benefits beyond the narrow framework of Rome, Italy and the Mediterranean fringe. For the empire to thrive, its provincials must be given a sense of belonging, to be made to feel secure, and encouraged to turn their thoughts inwards. Hadrian's Wall and other, similar frontiers, were one means of achieving this ideal.

That the barrier was as much symbolic as functional cannot be doubted (**46**). Roman practice elsewhere was to keep careful watch on potential hostile build-up beyond the frontier. In this area, too, there were doubtless contacts with friendly tribes to the north, and the political situation would be carefully monitored through such intelligence reports as were available. In addition, there were outpost forts retained in the land north of the Wall. Rapid communication, and possibly a chain of signalling beacons, would be required from them back to wall-posts. One such is Bewcastle, an irregularly-shaped fort, surprisingly remote, even today, and never commanding very extensive views of the surrounding countryside. The fort was fitted onto its plateau-top, and is dated by the find of an inscription recording the Emperor Hadrian and two of the legions who built the Wall. Excavations have revealed only a little of the Hadrianic layout, with the exception of the baths, placed unusually within the ramparts, but, despite its odd shape, the fort still had a headquarters building at its centre, and the commandant's house next to it. Though built in Hadrianic times, the fort was maintained in occupation, perhaps not continually, until the fourth century. Other outpost forts apparently also occupied in the Hadrianic period were Netherby and Birrens. All three, concentrated towards the western end of the Wall, may indicate that the main threat was expected to come from that direction. In later phases, too, the Wall was supplemented by other outposts along the major road routes northwards, some of them on the sites of earlier forts established in the wake of Agricola's advance into the north, but others in completely new locations.

So much for the Wall as originally planned, but it did not for long remain solely a barrier with milecastles and turrets. Strategic planners soon discovered, perhaps, that the barrier not only prevented progress by barbarians from the north into the Roman province, but also hampered the movement of Roman troops in the area beyond the Wall. Two improvements were clearly desirable. One was the improvement of access through the Wall by troops, the other, the strengthening of the number of men in permanent stations on the frontier itself, by the addition of forts to the wall-line.

Mobility had always been important for the Roman army, and the erection of this barrier which provided a single gateway to the north at each mile may have seriously impeded tactical manoeuvres. The placing of forts on the Wall — installations which housed more men than the milecastles and other Wall structures could ever have hoped to do — allowed far more gates to issue forth north of the Wall, and provided the men to make use of them. Most of the primary forts added to the Wall have three of their main double gates opening north of the Wall's line, and only one to its south. This in itself suggests that Roman strategists were having second thoughts about the defensive attitude revealed by the Wall: even if not used in anger, the barrier required a more aggressive stance, and the forts appear to have supplied it.

The other side of the coin is the availability of more men for sorties and expeditions than had been the case with the restricted garrisons of the milecastles. Where all the units came from to man the sixteen eventual forts is not known. Garrisons appear to have been continually on the move in northern Britain in the Trajanic and early Hadrianic periods and there was a shifting pattern of occupancy and refurbishment in many of the so-called 'hinterland' forts in the Pennines and the Lake District during this period. Of the early garrisons known to have been stationed at Wall forts, several seem to have been either of cavalry or are deduced to have been a mixed garrison of cavalry and infantry, implying that rapid deployment was at a premium. No clear indications are given about the level of occupancy of the milecastles after the forts were added to the Wall: one might have assumed that with the addition of forts — a far more comfortable and permanent billet for troops — the milecastles' function of accommodating men might have dwindled. They can never have been very attractive places to live, but all the indications are that they were occupied despite the presence of troops in the forts, and that they remained in occupation during the life of the Wall, some of them with a bewilderingly complex series of rebuilt barracks or other accommodation inside them. The indications are, therefore, of a strengthening of the number of troops on the Wall: Corbridge fort, at any rate, seems to be one of those which were abandoned at this moment, with its *Ala Petriana* possibly moved on to the Wall line.

The balance between defensive barrier and offensive capability thus remedied, the final, and least explicable part of the scheme was now

47 *Hadrian's Wall and the vallum at Limestone corner from the air. The modern road (B 6318) runs straight up the centre of the picture: immediately to its right, in deep shadow, is the Wall ditch, except for a short stretch nearest the camera where the Wall and its ditch swing away from the road to the right. At the foot of the picture, the small earthwork remains of milecastle 30 can be seen: its platform is crossed by a field wall. To the left of the road, the Vallum, its south mound interrupted at regular intervals, deviates slightly from the road's line.*

added. Once troops were moved up on to the Wall, contact between garrisons was now more important than it had been before, and although the forts were linked to the Stanegate as the main east–west route, easier intercommunication near the Wall line was desirable. At a later stage this was to be provided by a new military road closer to the Wall, but some sort of east–west track was also provided in association with the earthwork, to the south of the forts, known as the vallum (**47**).

This was not the vallum's main function, however, which seems to have been to act as a barrier to restrict access to the wall from the south. It was not as heavily or as constantly defended perhaps as the wall itself, but it still formed a formidable obstacle. Unlike the Wall ditch, which was left unfinished in places owing to the difficulty of cutting through solid rock, the vallum was completed even in those places, as at the northernmost point of the Wall, at Limestone Corner, where the Wall ditch was not (**48**). Apparently only at the forts was it easily possible to cross the vallum and here the crossing point was guarded by a gate.

If the Wall had cut off mobility to the north by the provision of a gateway only every mile or so, the vallum formed an even more severe restriction for progress to or from the south. Between Wallsend and Newcastle, where the river Tyne effectively blocked any penetration into the Wall zone, the vallum was not provided. But troops were now stationed in force in this

48 *The rock-cut Wall ditch at Limestone corner, showing the size of some of the blocks left in the ditch and never removed by the Roman soldiers and stonecutters.*

military zone defined by the vallum. With its construction, their rear was made doubly safe, and they were set on a positively forward footing despite the barrier to forward movement imposed by Hadrian's Wall.

The reasons for securing the rearward in this way are not known. One can of course speculate that internal resistance to the construction of the Wall was unexpectedly fierce, and that there had been a miscalculation of the reaction by the Brigantes to their contacts with the north being cut off. Although it began as a control across the frontier zone to ensure that access by barbarians or other undesirables was limited, the barrier had clearly evolved into something rather different, perhaps within ten years. Pressures from the south, not the north, were now firmly held in check by the vallum, not itself a defended barrier, but a marker which delimited military territory. At the same time, the war footing for troops on the Wall line was made more positive: they clearly faced forward. All the forts which could do so faced north — their main gates issuing beyond the wall. The whole construction now seemed even more self-confident than before. If the vallum cut off access from the south, it also cut off retreat in that direction too, and its addition to the scheme clearly indicates that there was no intention of retreat. Tactically speaking, if the Romans were under positive or unremitting threat from the north, the vallum was a mistake.

The situation did alter after Hadrian, when the Roman armies once more did begin to push northwards and into southern Scotland in a further attempt to annexe the territory between the Tyne–Solway and the Forth–Clyde estuaries. There must have been tactical reasons for this, and perhaps the stability which the construction of Hadrian's frontier had ensured was sufficient to reawaken dreams of conquest in this zone. Tactical and strategic considerations were altering all the time in this area. The archaeological picture provided by the construction of the Wall and its subsequent additions and revisions shows that shifts of emphasis were continually possible. In probably no more than a decade since its conception, the Wall had altered from a control measure to a potential springboard, ever watchful, but taut and prepared, positive rather than negative. The frontier had crystallised in the form set by Hadrian, but its shape was still capable of changing.

6

Abandonment and reoccupation

Hadrian's frontier had reached almost its full complexity by the time of its author's death in 138. Within only a couple of years, however, the new emperor Antoninus Pius had formulated a different plan which involved pushing Roman forces once more northwards in a further attempt to occupy and hold lowland Scotland. Antoninus' biographer puts what happened relatively succinctly: 'now he constrained the Britons through his legate Lollius Urbicus by building another wall of turf, and removing the barbarians...'. Inscriptions confirm the presence of Lollius Urbicus on the northern frontier. He built stone granaries in the fort at Corbridge in AD 139–40, and carried out rebuilding at the fort of High Rochester on Dere Street. Both of these were clearly part of the supporting role for the move northwards.

The Antonine Wall, built of turf, was established between Carriden on the Firth of Forth and Old Kilpatrick, just west of Glasgow, on the Clyde (**49**). It was 40 Roman miles (58 km) in length and was built of turf on a clay and cobble base and fronted by a ditch. Indications are that it was probably about 10 ft (3 m) high, the same height as the turf wall at the western end of Hadrian's Wall, and that there was a breastwork of wattles — recent finds suggest perhaps of willow and ash — at its top. The

49 *The Antonine Wall and its forts in Roman Scotland. The forts are: 1 Bishopton 2 Old Kilpatrick 3 Duntocher 4 Cleddans (fortlet) 5 Castlehill 6 Bearsden 7 Summerston 8 Balmuildy 9 Wilderness plantation (fortlet) 10 Cadder 11 Glasgow Bridge (fortlet) 12 Kirkintilloch 13 Auchendavy 14 Bar Hill 15 Croy Hill 16 Westerwood 17 Castlecary 18 Seabegs (fortlet) 19 Rough Castle 20 Watling Lodge (fortlet) 21 Camelon 22 Falkirk 23 Mumrills 24 Inveravon 25 Kinneil (fortlet) 26 Carriden.*

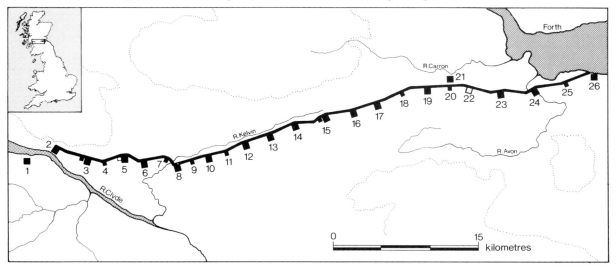

frontier of Hadrian's Wall grew more complex by stages, and the Antonine Wall appears to be no different. Current research has it that it began as a turf barrier with six forts, the largest on its line, spaced at about 8-mile (11 km) intervals. Evidence is beginning to be found for a series of milecastles or fortlets attached to the Wall, in a plan that makes them look almost exactly like the milecastles of Hadrian's Wall. One, excavated most recently at Kinneil, is almost an exact parallel to the Turf Wall milecastle at High House on Hadrian's frontier. As yet, only nine such 'milecastles' are known for certain on the Antonine Wall.

Relatively soon after its beginning, a further decision which led to the siting of more forts on the line of this wall was taken. At least a further twenty forts were added to the Wall's line, in an operation which made it the most intensively occupied frontier line for its length in the Roman world. Most of the forts were of turf and timber like the wall to which they were attached, and often with an annexe, also walled off in turf, attached to them. Their internal buildings were normally of timber, but the annexe often contained a bath-house, usually the only building to be constructed of stone.

This new wall and its forts were mainly built by the three legions stationed in Britain who had also built Hadrian's Wall some twenty years earlier together with the support of some auxiliary units in the area. Their efforts are recorded in a remarkable series of stone inscriptions which record in detail the precise length of the new barrier built by each legion, as well as by a number of building inscriptions which show that auxiliary troops were engaged in the fort building. These appear to have been set up at each end of a legionary building length; at the eastern end, perhaps where work began, the length assigned to each legion was 4666 *passus*, or four and two thirds Roman miles, though there are slight variations in the amount of building claimed by different legions. At the western end of the Wall, the lengths are nearly a third of this distance, perhaps signifying a rather more hasty completion of the task by splitting the available manpower into smaller sections. The distance slab from Bridgeness, at the eastern end of the Wall, set up by the *legio II Augusta* is perhaps the most elaborate. It shows the Romans triumphing over barbarian captives as well as the sacrifice marking the

end of a successful campaign. Not all are quite as decorative as this but the fact that as many as eighteen of these slabs have survived in relatively good condition suggests that they may not have been left in place by the Romans when the Antonine Wall was finally abandoned, but deliberately concealed so as to avoid their re-use or desecration.

Of the many vexed questions about this episode of Roman military occupation of the north, one of the most difficult to address is the reason for the construction of the Antonine Wall and the abandonment of the barrier established by Hadrian. By the end of his reign, Hadrian's Wall could be seen as not so much a negative barrier but as a springboard for further movement northwards for, with troops now mounted on the Wall, fort gateways affording easy access beyond it, and the vallum protecting the rearward, its main thrust was now turned in this direction. The answers to why the Antonine Wall was built must be sought, however, either in political manoeuvring or in tactical necessity.

Antoninus Pius' biographer mentions barbarians who were removed and a potential situation in Britain which required strong action. It is possible that tribes from beyond the Wall were building up pressure at this time. An enigmatic sentence by the Greek writer Pausanias mentions that the emperor deprived the Brigantes of most of their territory because of an invasion they had made into a district which cannot be identified but which clearly according to Roman opinion did not belong to them. If the territory of the Brigantes stretched to the north of Hadrian's Wall as well as to its south, the occupation of lowland Scotland could be seen as a punitive measure of this sort, but the scale of the Roman advance into Scotland in 139–40 was far greater and more permanent than a mere reprisal or punitive campaign.

Perhaps more likely was the need of Antoninus Pius, like Claudius before him, to register a success, particularly in the form of new territory for the empire. Already by 140–2, his coins carried the portrait of Britannia, signifying that he was claiming some success in the province. But even if undertaken primarily for military prestige, the campaign clearly was a thorough exercise in control and in establishing once more the security of the northern line. Nor was the Antonine Wall the absolute limit of Roman control even now: beyond it lay a road leading out into the Tay basin, with further forts strung out along it, at Camelon, Ardoch, Strageath and Bertha. It seems clear, however, that the concentrations of forces along the new Wall, perhaps completed by about 145, switched the balance of control to the northern wall and once more left the way open for southern Scotland, the area between the two Walls, to become part of the British provinces.

The effects of this new advance on the installations of Hadrian's Wall itself are hard to gauge. It might be expected that Hadrian's frontier was completely abandoned, but this does not seem entirely to have been the case. The fort at Corbridge was now rebuilt again, perhaps because of is focal position on the supply route up Dere Street for other positions further north. Carlisle, too, may have provided the same function for the western route. Two inscriptions of the period from Chesters, however, show that this fort at least still had a function and a garrison. This gives a pointer to the possibility that others of the Hadrian's Wall forts too may have been retained in use.

Milecastles and turrets, however, appear to have fared differently. The milecastles, which provided gateways through the Wall, appear to have had their actual gates totally removed. At milecastle 48, excavations revealed that the stones which held the gate pivots were broken: only thus was it possible to remove the gates which turned in iron collars set into sockets in the gate thresholds. A similar sequence of events has been recorded at other milecastles, suggesting that in some cases at least the doors were physically removed from their seating, and that access through Hadrian's Wall was left unobstructed. This cannot be seen to have happened at fort gateways, however, and the forts therefore may not have been treated in the same way. With the establishment of another frontier some 90 miles (150 km) to the north of Hadrian's Wall, the surveillance function of the turrets was no longer necessary, and these, too, appear to have been abandoned – if they were ever in permanent occupation.

The impression gained from this is that the Hadrianic frontier was still manned, though perhaps not so intensively as before. Excavation would have to be carried out comprehensively at a good many Wall-forts to establish precisely which of them suffered a break in occupation around AD 140, particularly, as will be seen, since this break was to last for only

about twenty-five years at the most. The firm dating of coins and, above all, pottery from deposits within sites on the Wall can rarely be guaranteed unless the assemblages are rich and contain a number of distinctive pottery types in sufficient numbers. In archaeological terms a gap of twenty-five years in occupation might be difficult to tell apart from a gap of several months. However, there is evidence in the 140s for a change in garrison in some of the Hadrian's Wall forts. The auxiliary units for which they had been built were pushed northwards, and detachments of legionaries moved in. It has not been possible to study the changes in fort barracks which might be a sign of their alterations in garrison except in one or two places, none of them areas where the presence of legionary troops is attested. It is of course possible that a change in garrison did not automatically mean a change in buildings — new troops might move in and adopt existing buildings to their needs without massive structural alterations.

The change in character of Hadrian's Wall, from control point to support role, is also reflected in the treatment of the vallum. In some areas, the vallum ditch and its accompanying mounds were deliberately backfilled and levelled at regular intervals to enable unrestricted passage to and from the former militarised zone. On Cockmount Hill, where these causeways through the vallum occur at about 130 ft (40 m) intervals, excavation showed that the crossing had been formed after a certain amount of weathering of the vallum ditches had taken place, and after the establishment of plant species which one might have expected to colonise cleared ground within about five to fifteen years. If this can be taken as an accurate indicator, therefore, it suggests that in this zone at least, and by implication, in others where the same sequence occurs, the provision of multiple causeways across the vallum was made around 140–5.

Short of total dismantling, therefore, Hadrian's Wall seems to have been rendered impotent as a barrier, though the evidence for this is piecemeal, and what can be shown to have happened in one stretch of the barrier which stretched for 80 miles (117 km) need not have happened everywhere. On the Solway coast, for example, the conditions may still have been substantially different from those in the central sector, where the line of posts along the Stanegate, supplemented by legionary detachments at places like Chesters, Benwell and Housesteads, maintained an adequate Roman military presence.

Evidence for events on the northern frontiers in the 150s is hard to string together into anything coherent. Britannia, the symbol or embodiment of the province, appears on coins struck in 154–5, but what event in the province this commemorated is uncertain. Detachments of the three British legions and of other legions from Germany set up an inscription at Newcastle at about this time, but the reasons for their presence there, or what they commemorated, are not known. But there is an inscription, carefully dated to 158, which records work by the sixth legion probably to repair or rebuild the curtain wall of Hadrian's Wall itself between milecastles 11 and 13. This suggests that Hadrian's Wall was once again by the later years of the decade considered of importance.

The date at which the Antonine Wall was abandoned in favour of a return to Hadrian's Wall has been extensively sought and argued over. Study of the glossy red Roman pottery — Samian ware — from sites on both Hadrian's Wall and the Antonine Wall shows that there are striking differences in detail between the two. Few of the potters whose wares were reaching the Antonine Wall were also supplying material to sites on Hadrian's Wall. If the supply of pottery to the army was centrally organised, this suggests that there is a chronological difference between the occupation of the two Walls. In addition, evidence from several of the Antonine Wall forts shows some replanning and reconstruction of interior buildings. These scraps of evidence, perhaps of dubious value when taken singly, have the cumulative effect of suggesting that the Antonine Wall was abandoned around 157–8, after only fifteen years of occupation at the most. New finds of pottery groups from well excavated and dateable buildings on Hadrian's Wall — for example at recent excavations at Wallsend, Housesteads, South Shields or Birdoswald — may alter this picture. More comprehensive evidence could show that there is a greater overlap. Nor, archaeologically, is it easy to define the exact date of the interruption of occupation in the Antonine Wall forts, but the best evidence available at present, taken with the inscription of 158 which shows rebuilding on Hadrian's Wall, indicates a return to Hadrian's frontier by the end of the 150s. Some

forts in the Scottish lowlands, in particular Netherby and Birrens, have also produced evidence of an interruption in occupation at about this time.

For an interruption was all it was. Within only a very short space of time Birrens and Netherby were rebuilt, and demolished and evacuated buildings in Antonine Wall forts were under reconstruction. Once again, study of the die-stamps with which individual potters signed their names on Samian ware has shown that the renewed occupation of the Antonine Wall was extremely brief, and that by 163 or so, the Scottish frontier had been given up, this time finally. Only at a few of the outpost forts north of Hadrian's Wall, notably Newstead and Birrens once more, did later occupation continue.

The reasons for this apparent vacillation in frontier policy are hard to divine. It has been suggested that there was internal trouble in northern England in the mid 160s, but the evidence for this is weak. Policy changes of themselves are not impossible — witness the constant alterations to Hadrian's Wall during the course of its construction — and the abandonment of the Antonine Wall followed by its immediate reoccupation could be no more than answers to changing military perceptions of the strategic needs in the north. Alternatively, the extent of territory held and fully garrisoned in the north will always have been dependent upon the manpower available, and there is evidence of withdrawals of troops from Britain to fight in the war in the later 150s against the Chatti in Germany. If withdrawals took place, the Antonine frontier may have seemed overextended, and the see-sawing between the two northern frontiers could be a product, at least in part, of the deployment of available manpower resources not entirely dependant on the situation in Britain alone.

The Roman world was under threat at the beginning of the reign of Marcus Aurelius in 161 from the Parthians in the east, and from the Chatti in Germany. There appears, too, to have been a gathering storm in Britain, and the arrival of a new governor, Sextus Calpurnius Agricola, soon resulted in the decision to concentrate on the Hadrianic frontier. Inscriptions from Corbridge, Carvoran and Vindolanda, all of them significantly Stanegate rather than Hadrian's Wall sites, supply the evidence for the new governor's role in rebuilding sites by

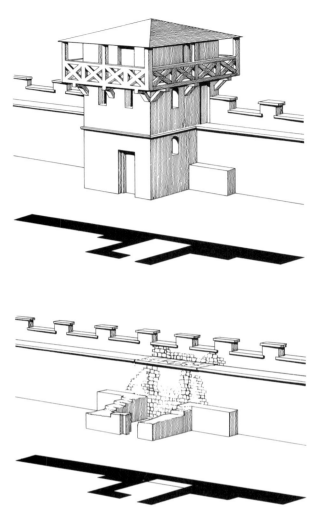

50 *The suppression of a turret: a sketch sequence of the way in which turrets were removed from the wall.*

trans vallum prospere gestas — vallum being the Latin term for Hadrian's frontier, not just the earthwork we know as the vallum; and a tombstone from the fort at Ambleside, difficult to date, but possibly from this period, records the death of someone at the fort through enemy action. Guerrilla warfare may therefore have been a constant threat, and the Hadrianic frontier was manned again to avert at least the most hostile of the northern adversaries.

Changes now took place to Hadrian's Wall. We must assume that milecastles were provided with new gateways where they had originally been thrown open. The wall curtain itself was rebuilt, or, in those places where it may still never have been completed, work will have concentrated afresh on building it. Some reassessment of the role of the turrets was clearly also undertaken, for in certain cases they were dismantled and the portion which had been recessed into the line of Hadrian's Wall was filled up solid with masonry (**50**). At turret 33b, Coesyke (**51**), the impression gained by the excavations was that there were so few finds of anything other than the earliest Hadrianic period as to suggest that this process happened in the later 160s. In the process, a building inscription recording work by the sixth legion was used, inscribed side inwards, as part of the extra masonry required to re-establish the full width of Hadrian's Wall. The dating evidence for this change, however, which affected a number of the turrets in the central sector, does not afford any certainty as to when this change in the planning and provision of turrets took place. In some cases this could equally well have been undertaken around fifty years later.

There is also a lack of clear evidence for what new dispositions may have been made at milecastles at this time. At Sewingshields, where excavation revealed at least six phases of altering internal layouts, the Hadrianic plan, which comprised a small stone building in one corner, possibly supplemented by other timber buildings, seems to have undergone some slight refurbishment, but the excavators were not able to identify any thoroughgoing alteration of the layout at this stage (see **81**, p. 107). Analysis of the pottery from the site, however, has shown quite clearly that vessels of the later second century are well represented, and suggest strongly that the site was in occupation and use at this period.

At the western end of the Wall there were

then either lightly held or unoccupied. This evidence must date from around 162 or the years immediately afterwards. Further building or rebuilding work is attested in the late 160s at Stanwix and on Hadrian's Wall itself, and there was also rebuilding at the forts of Ilkley and Ribchester, deeper in the Pennines.

When Lucius Verus, co-opted by Marcus Aurelius as his co-emperor, died in 169, Britain was still reportedly on the brink of war. It is difficult to tell how this pressure, perceived at Rome, might have made itself felt on the frontier itself. An altar west of Carlisle was dedicated by a legate of the sixth legion because of a 'successful campaign beyond the frontier' — *ob res*

51 *Turret 33b (Coesike), from the west. The turret had short wing-walls of broad gauge, but Hadrian's Wall when it was built in this sector was narrower. At a later stage, the turret fell into disuse, and the portion of Wall which had been narrowed to form the interior of the turret was filled up with masonry. In this picture, this has clearly dipped into softer ground.*

more changes. At some stage, the whole portion of the Wall originally built in turf, from the crossing of the River Irthing to the end of the Wall at Bowness, a distance of some 31 Roman miles, was converted to stone. This included the sites of the six forts from Birdoswald to Bowness. The sequence of events at Birdoswald is the most complicated (**52**): the fort was planned, as we have already seen, to lie astride the turf wall to cover the site of the stone turret 49b. Excavations in and around the southern defences of the fort suggested that a complex series of smaller camps or enclosures, perhaps the labour camps for troops building the fort and the remainder of the defensive scheme, lay in the neighbourhood, but were all abandoned

by the time, around AD 130, that the vallum was built to run round the southern edge of the fort. The stone-built fort at Birdoswald lies in the same relationship to the turf wall as other forts elsewhere do to the stone wall, with its northern third projecting to the north of it. This suggests that the turf wall was still in existence when the fort was planted here. Later, however, when the turf wall was removed and a stone wall substituted, in order to allow more space in very restricted ground around the southern flanks of the fort, the new stone wall did not follow the line which had been taken by the turf one. Instead of joining the stone fort at the main east and west gates, it now butted up to the fort's northernmost corners (**53**). West of Birdoswald, this new stone barrier wall was continued on an entirely different line from the turf wall for about 2 miles (3½ km): new turrets, and a new milecastle, number 50, had to be built, but still reflected the same system and spacing as before.

For the remainder of its course, the turf wall was replaced in stone: turrets, already built of stone, were incorporated within this replace-

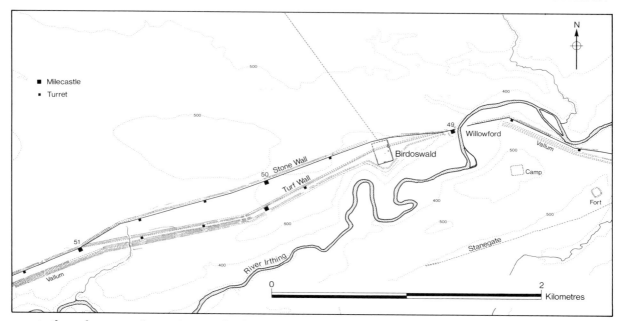

- ■ Milecastle
- ● Turret

52 *The Birdoswald area. The map shows about three miles of Wall west of the crossing of the River Irthing at Willowford. It includes the stretch of Turf Wall west of milecastle 49, at Harrow's Scar, which was not later followed by the stone Wall. Although the fort at Birdoswald is in a conventional relationship to the turf wall, with three of its gates projecting beyond it, the later stone wall takes a more northerly line, affording more space round the fort on a restricted plateau. Turf wall milecastles 50 and 51, and all their intervening turrets, were abandoned when the stone wall was built, and stone substitutes were added to the new stone wall.*

ment, though some adaptation to the height of the first floor doorways may have been required. Milecastles were built in stone on the site of their turf and timber predecessors. As the sequence of events around Birdoswald shows, there are a number of stages which have to be allotted time within the sequence of events. Further evidence comes from turret 54a, where the primary stone turret attached to the Turf wall had collapsed into the ditch. A second one, still apparently built as part of the turf wall, was placed behind its site and was occupied. Later the stone wall was brought up to the turret on both sides, and at a final stage, the turret was dismantled and the wall continued over its site.

A further addition to the wall scheme made at this time was a road linking all its elements. Known now as the 'military way', this road ran from fort to fort within the area bounded by the Wall and the vallum and clearly postdates the construction of the vallum, since in some places it runs along its north mound. In others, it veers nearer the Wall: at Housesteads, for example, the road is the track which strikes out westwards from the west gate of the fort. Aerial photographs in places show the traces of smaller paths linking this road to elements of the Wall: at turret 37a, where the turret, like others, was eventually obliterated, traces of such a track have been spotted on aerial photographs. Thus the road dates from after the

vallum's construction around 130, and before the time, somewhere between then and AD 160–200, that some of the turrets were demolished and the Wall built over their sites. Despite all the changes and improvements to Hadrian's Wall which took place either now or within the next fifty years, however, there is no sign that the vallum was put back into fully working order. Some areas where gaps were forced through the mounds and material filled the ditch to make causeways were left in that state.

Part at least of the reason for this may have been the growth of settlements of civilians outside the forts on the Wall, beside those along the Stanegate frontier and possibly, too, in association with some of the forts further north. This whole aspect of the frontier will be dealt

77

53 *Hadrian's Wall east of Birdoswald. The southern side of this stretch of Wall from the fort at Birdoswald to milecastle 49 at Harrow's Scar, above the River Irthing, contains a good number of crudely inscribed stones recording work-lengths undertaken by individual* centuriae.

with in more detail in the next chapter, but the presence of troops with money to spend will have acted as a considerable magnet to those in a position to provide local services. Clusters of camp-followers of all kinds will have followed the army around, and gradually such clusters formed into shanty towns, shanty-towns into grander accommodation, all increasing in permanence in a measure similar to that of the forts themselves. A recent reassessment of the coin evidence for the settlement at Vindolanda has suggested that the earliest *vicus* or 'village' outside the fort's west gate may have belonged to Hadrian's reign. This first *vicus* — a series of long buildings fronting onto a main street, and incorporating the fort's bath-house within what appears to have been a defended enclosure — was occupied up until at least 180, and a second, much more enlarged settlement was established later, perhaps not until the early third century.

Similar developments may have been taking place elsewhere, particularly at those forts where occupation by Roman troops during the move up to the Antonine Wall in the 140s to 150s was more or less continuous. Already the gradual process of demilitarisation of the army had begun: its traces are visible in the archaeological record in the silting of the vallum ditch at Benwell and other forts, the sprawl of buildings belonging to the settlements over the forgotten vallum's remains, the dedication in around 180 of an altar to the god Antenociticus at the small temple outside the fort, or the beginning and flowering in the second century at Carrawburgh of the cult of the water goddess Coventina and her well, only a stone's throw from the fort ramparts. The most spectacular development, more significant than all these, is the conversion of the site at Corbridge from a military fort to a garrison town, with a complete change in layout and the use of its buildings. Doubtless, a similar development took place at Carlisle, converting the earlier fort into a more fully fledged town, though, buried as this now is under the modern city, its traces are more hard to find.

Events on the northern frontier during the remainder of the second century bear a close relationship with the fate of the remainder of the province. In 180 the new emperor Commodus faced what may have been the most serious situation yet in Britain. The tribes in the island, we are told, had crossed the wall that separated them from the Roman forts. They did a great deal of damage, killing a general (perhaps the provincial governor himself) and the troops he had with him. Commodus was alarmed, and sent Ulpius Marcellus against them. By 184 Commodus had accepted the honorary title *Britannicus* which is an indication of some success to be claimed in the island, and coins of that and the following year proclaim a 'British victory'. Marcellus is mentioned on two building stones from Chesters set up by its new unit, the second wing of the Asturian cavalry, one of which records the provision of an aqueduct for the fort (**54**).

The murder of Commodus in 192, followed within a year by the murder of his successor as emperor, Pertinax, threw the empire into confusion and civil war. Armies from three sectors of the empire pushed forward their own candidates for imperial power: from the Danubian armies came Septimius Severus, from the east Pescennius Niger, and from Britain the governor Clodius Albinus. Severus, the nearest to Rome, reached the capital first and was proclaimed emperor, but the rival candidates had to be headed off. By offering Albinus the

dubious title of Caesar, Severus gained time to confront Niger. After defeating him, and with his position the stronger, he was able to turn his attention to Clodius Albinus. Outmanoeuvred and somewhat isolated in Britain, Albinus now decided to gather his forces and march towards Rome for the decisive battle. He crossed into Gaul, attempted to win the Rhine legions over to his side, though in fact they remained firmly neutral, and met Severus' forces near Lyons. Albinus was defeated, and shortly afterwards, he himself was killed.

What provision he made for the northern frontier — or indeed any of the defences of Britain — before withdrawing troops to fight on his behalf is not known. It is likely that he

54 *A fragmentary inscription from Chesters fort recording the loyal declaration of its unit, that 'while the emperors are safe, the* Ala II Augusta *is happy'. The date seems to be* AD 221–2, *when two emperors reigned together (note the double 'G' to signify two Augusti), one of whom later suffered* damnatio memoriae *and was erased from the record. The third line of the inscription is missing, and may have contained an honorific title linked to the missing emperor (Severus Alexander). Beneath the inscription is part of the depiction of the unit's standards.*

took with him all those troops considered to have the necessary mobility to fight an active campaign, though this may not have extended to garrison troops on frontier postings. Certainly in the one case we know of, the garrison at Chesters which was in post at the fort in the 180s was also there in later centuries, suggesting that it was not moved in the disruption caused by this internal strife. Other Hadrian's Wall forts may have remained equally untouched by events elsewhere. The only indication, however, that there was further trouble is given in a reference to the years between 197 and 200, when the new governor, Virius Lupus, was forced to buy peace from a tribe called the Maeatae for a great sum of money, since the Caledonians did not keep their promises to Rome and were threatening to assist them. On the strength of this statement, which must refer to the prospect of serious trouble from the Scottish tribes if not an outright confrontation, it has been suggested that the Maeatae had taken advantage of the lack of watchfulness on the frontier caused by the pretensions of Albinus to imperial power. This, it has been claimed, led to destruction of several Wall sites, and to the hostile presence of these unwelcome tribesmen south of the frontier, and the consequent need of the Romans to buy them off at great cost.

There is in fact little evidence that this supposed invasion took place. Rebuilding of northern sites is attested by inscriptions which Virius Lupus had set up at the forts at Ilkley, Bowes and Corbridge, but this is hardly a sign that there had been a widespread disaster and invasion. Nor is the payment of subsidy to maintain the peace anything particularly new, though in this case, the scale of payment was clearly such as to excite comment. It became an established Roman practice to control buffer states outside the empire's bounds, through subsidy and other kinds of encouragement. In this way those immediately outside the imperial boundaries could be relied on to act as early warning of serious threat, and to absorb the initial ferocity of any hostile intentions from outsiders. In addition, the position just outside Rome's borders, which allowed independence but a measure of reliable economic interchange, was one which would be jealously guarded, and any unwelcome threats from outside which might jeopardise the established equilibrium of co-existence would be repelled all the more readily.

A state of affairs such as this may underlie the agreement which the Caledonians were failing to keep, but is not a sure sign that there was hostile action. Nearly forty years had passed since the abandonment of the Antonine Wall, and Hadrian's frontier was now beginning to crystallise in what was to become its final form. Severus had now defeated all other pretenders to imperial power, and was established on the throne. Together with his sons Caracalla and Geta, he ushered in the prospect of further stability to come.

7

Civilians on the Wall

The presence in northern Britain of a military force for upwards of 300 years is a break, albeit a substantial one, in the background patterns of settlement and agriculture of the region which had been forming for millennia before the Roman army's arrival. In earlier chapters we have already had occasion to consider the political or strategic considerations which may have compelled the Roman commanders to enter the area in the first place, to choose this or that location for a fort or watchtower, or to begin the construction of the linear frontier works. These are areas where the Roman military forces might most naturally come up short against the native inhabitants of the region and see them as a politically sensitive population which required firm control or policing.

This cannot, however, be the whole story from either side. From the Roman viewpoint, it was impossible for them to remain for so long in an area which was positively and continuously hostile to the army's presence. The resources required for constant campaigning, the supply of food and equipment for a large standing army, and the sheer logistics of military provisions of all kinds demanded that ways be found of establishing reasonable relations with nearby peoples. From the point of view of those who lived in the area before the Romans arrived, once the original resentment of the presence of an occupying force had worked itself out by a continuing familiarity, there were opportunities to profit in material terms from the proximity of the Roman army. Troops themselves had some money to spend and there were luxury goods to be had. In this way, we may expect that a form of interdependence ought to have built up.

Stated thus baldly, the proposition looks sim-

ple. It is far more difficult to prove, either from documentary or archaeological evidence, what kind of relationship there was between Roman and native. The topic is a large and complex one and it is possible here only to touch on some aspects of the problems it raises. To understand the Roman frontier zone, it is important to have some grasp of the development of patterns of local settlement in the area prior to the Roman period, and to assess the extent of any changes which can be detected in these patterns as a result of the Roman arrival. Some consideration must also be given to the demands of the Roman army in the frontier region, and the extent to which these could be expected to be met locally. Third, no Roman fort appears to have been planted for long on British soil before it had attracted a sprawling settlement outside its gates: where did such settlements spring from, and what part did their inhabitants play in the mixture of army contacts with native people? Finally, no work on Hadrian's Wall would be complete without at least a brief examination of the major Roman towns in the region, Carlisle, and, in particular, Corbridge, which perhaps more than anything provides the key to some of the Roman aspirations for the region in general.

There is some evidence to suggest that by about 400 BC, the climate was improving sufficiently in the north of England so as to encourage the settlement, exploitation and clearance of forest from lowland areas. Some 400 years earlier than this, however, a deterioration in climatic conditions had meant the abandonment of many of the upland areas, and the concentration of settlements at lower levels and on more favourable sites than hitherto. Settlement sites surrounded by palisades, probably for defence, are relatively common at this early date, and were in many cases succeeded by later prehistoric hillforts. Such settlements normally enclosed a single round house of timber, which may have held accommodation for a single family or a large nucleated group. By 400 BC, palisaded homesteads seem to have gone increasingly out of fashion, perhaps because timber was becoming scarcer, and larger 'hillforts' with more substantial defences took their place. Some of these, such as the hillfort on Yeavering Bell, are large and clearly formed a major settlement, whereas others, surrounded only by a single simple ditch, are far smaller, and represent perhaps a single

55 *Traces of pre-Roman ploughing uncovered at Denton, near Newcastle, just to the south of the remains of Hadrian's Wall, and sealed beneath the Roman ground surfaces.*

farmstead. Huts within these settlements were still round, and still mainly of timber.

Often both the larger and the smaller sites gained significant improvements to their defences as time went by, and most of the larger ones ended up with more than one ring of ramparts. Such places may have formed the permanent home for a small family or clan group of political or social elite. From them an essentially agricultural community could be run, making use of the uplands for pasture and the valley bottoms for agriculture. Stockyards, apparently mainly for cattle, were often added to the main house or enclosure.

Particular concentrations of settlements of this type, enclosed by circular or rectangular ditches, are known in the Northumberland coastal plans as well as in part of Cumbria. Without excavation, these are very difficult to date either to the late Iron Age or to the Roman period, and most of those which have been excavated have displayed some continuity of

56 *Earthworks of the settlement at Ewe Close, Cumbria. A central circular farmstead, consisting of at least one hut circle and surrounding yards, has grown in three directions to form other subsidiary yards containing further round houses and fields.*

occupation throughout this whole era. Arable farming as well as a pastoral economy was important, and it is, ironically, beneath the remains of Hadrian's Wall and its forts that the evidence of this has often survived best. Signs of pre-Roman ploughing have come from beneath the forts at Wallsend, Carrawburgh and Haltonchesters, as well as from relatively recent excavations under the Wall near Carlisle and at Denton, near Newcastle (**55**).

Analysis of pollens from northern sites found buried within soil samples taken from excavations suggests that during the Roman period the climate, and indeed the landscape, had reached very much the form it is in now. Deforestation was on the increase throughout the whole of the episode of Roman occupation. As far as local settlements are concerned there is no obvious disruption in settlement patterns which might have been caused by the Romans' arrival in the area in the later part of the first century AD. Two changes, however, can be noted. There was from this date an increasing number of settlements which were not enclosed by a ditch, palisade or any other obvious defensive feature (**56**); this was accompanied by the growth of a number of more nucleated groups of huts, in both Northumbria and Cumbria, which suggests both a new confidence in the peaceful conditions, and perhaps an expansion of the basic family or clan group (**57**).

One of the major problems in giving a chronological framework to any of these developments is that almost all of the sparse dating evidence available is in the form of Roman artefacts and pottery. There is in particular a marked concentration of second-century pottery on the native farmstead sites north of the Wall while later Roman material is only seldom found. This does not help to establish very clearly what date such settlements began to burgeon into this non-defensive and expanded form: was it as a consequence of the Romans' arrival, or was this a process which was already firmly in train by the first century AD? Much of the greatest impetus to contact between Roman and native came from the episodes during the second century when the frontier moved northwards into the lowland Scottish zone, and it is difficult to explain why this level of contact was not maintained from the time of Severus onwards. There is no evidence of depopulation in the northern areas in the third and fourth centuries, and considerable hints that not only

did the population stay put, but that the size of settlements continued to increase. On present evidence therefore, the Roman arrival in the north of England came at the same time as some stabilisation of social and climatic conditions which enabled the underlying population to be on the increase.

The scarcity of Roman artefacts, and of coins in particular, from the settlements north of the Wall in any but the second century poses problems about the nature of the Roman army's contacts with native farmers or clans. To some extent it must be true that some classes of Roman artefacts may have been of little interest to these folk. The possession of coinage was of little benefit to those outside the Roman world, but there ought to be more evidence of cross-cultural contact, for example in the provision of agricultural equipment, or of more exotic foodstuffs on native sites if peaceful or trading contacts between Romans and natives can be seen as significant.

If the Romans were forced to buy peace from the Maeatae in the years following AD 197, for example, they must have paid somehow. Quite apart from this, the presence of the army in the frontier zone must have placed a number of demands upon the surrounding area. There was a primary need for feeding a standing garrison of around 30,000 men, whose requirement would be around 10,000 tons of wheat a year, a figure which represents the yield of around 30,000 acres. Additionally, fodder was required for animals, including not only mounts for officers and cavalrymen, but also the pack and draught animals which the army required to keep it mobile. The staple ration of wheat was only one element of the Roman military diet which also encompassed a variety of vegetables, as well as meat when this too was available.

Besides these bulk supplies of food, the army had need of other official and private requisites: these included arms, armour, weapons and clothing, tools, leather for shoes, tents and other equipment, stone for building and metals of all kinds for equipment and repairs of existing gear. Many such supplies, once gathered, were retained for use for some considerable time: there is evidence that armour and weapons belonged to the unit and were issued against a stoppage of pay to a new recruit, before being handed back at the completion of a period of service and reissued anew. Armourer's hoards of material, collections of scrap metal and other

57 *Reconstruction view of the settlement at Milking Gap, just to the south of the Wall near Housesteads.*

useful objects such as those found at Corbridge (**colour plate 2**), suggest that keeping equipment in service by repair was the most cost-effective method of supplying the army's demands. Much of the new equipment required would be provided from specialist centres elsewhere — leatherwork from tanning factories or local cottage industries supplying the military market, clothing and armour from specialist manufacturing plants attested only in the fourth century but which surely also existed earlier. Some of the necessary materials could be won locally: stone, quarried for the Wall or for other buildings from nearby under military supervision, is the most obvious, while the need to keep watch over or provide accommodation for men engaged in the extraction of metals, lead, iron and silver, may have influenced the siting of several of the northern forts.

The extent to which supplies of foodstuffs for consumption either by the troops or their mounts might have been requisitioned, at fixed prices, from local sources cannot easily be determined. Evidence from other Roman frontiers suggests that most Roman forts were assigned a territory which formed an area for foraging for supplies for animals, and may also have included safe areas where valuable stock were kept corralled. It is one thing to guess that this must also have been the case in Britain, another to prove it. Some supplies of grain came from the Rhineland: the examination of samples from South Shields and the testimony of a fourth-century historian go to prove this, but grain was difficult and heavy to transport over long distances, and local requisitions may have been made in the central areas of the Wall in particular. The writing tablets from Vindolanda, dating from a century when affairs may not have been quite as they eventually settled down under Hadrian, record the receipt or issue of supplies of grain, mostly barley, as well as a list of foodstuffs which is far more exotic in content. It has been suggested that local overproduction of grain was encouraged to supply military needs in various areas.

58 *The fort and its* vicus *at Housesteads from the air. The Wall runs, almost in shadow, along the top of the crags towards the bottom of the picture, and strikes off from the fort's north-east (left-hand bottom) corner at an angle. Within the fort the outlines of its headquarters, the store-buildings below it, the commandant's house above, and the 'hospital' to its right are all clear. In the left hand corner of the fort are the traces of some of the barrack blocks, and elsewhere there are earthworks of others of its internal buildings. To the south and west of the fort in particular, the traces of its settlement, including individual buildings, and, to its right, what appear to be small rectangular fields or plot boundaries flanking the road running out of the west gate are sharply visible.*

The army was supported by taxation, which fell most naturally upon those who lay within the Roman province. While taxes were normally paid in cash, they could on occasion be commuted to payments in kind. One example is the levying of a tax on some frontier peoples in the first century reckoned in ox-hides, while some tribes were persuaded to provide recruits for the army in lieu of the payment of a monetary tax. The supply of fresh recruits for the army was a continuing and important need. Although the auxiliary troops on Hadrian's Wall may have been at first recruited elsewhere and though the unit may have a name which showed clearly where it had been originally raised — the cohort of Tungrians at Housesteads, for example, must originally have been raised from the area of Tongres in Belgium — once settled in Britain, they would scarcely have continued to recruit from precisely the same area. Local recruitment, however, is difficult to prove, but a career in military service offered much to a local youth, who, after around twenty-five years' service might expect to gain a modest pension, a small piece of land of his own, and the status of a Roman citizen, shared by himself and any children he might produce thereafter. British troops, named as '*Brittones*', are recorded in the second century on the Rhine frontier, and show that military service might take Britons out of their homeland as well as bring foreigners in.

The attractions of military service were not only the stability it offered, but the pay. Even after all the major stoppages which were automatically deducted, the soldier had some spare cash in his pocket every month, which must help to explain the proliferation outside the gates of virtually all Roman forts in the north of a sprawling settlement, known as a *vicus* (**58**). The area outside and round a fort was put to various uses which could not be accommodated within the camp: there was always a bathhouse,

and normally a number of temples and other quasi-official establishments such as a lodging house for official visitors where horses serving the imperial post, the communications network, might be stabled. Commonest of all, however, are the long narrow strip houses which may have served a variety of purposes — as shops, workshops, or perhaps domestic accommodation.

Soldiers on active service were not until the third century permitted to marry legally before retirement, but they may well have formed permanent liaisons with local women before that date, and doubtless children were born. Camp followers could therefore have included unofficial wives and families, and the settlement outside the walls was thus a place for trade and extra luxuries, for inns and other diversions,

59 *View of the changing-room of Chesters bathhouse. Part of the room's paved floor and six of the seven niches along its west wall can be seen. The entrance porch is to the right, and the doorway leading to the main treatment rooms of the bathhouse to the left, beyond the stone water trough in the centre of the room.*

both regular and illicit, for leisure and pleasure away from the duties of the fort.

The bathhouse was focal to the soldiers' off-duty hours. Bathing and keeping clean by a variety of steam and heat treatments was a discipline the Roman military establishment took seriously, and the complexity of the fort baths can be well seen at two places in the Wall region — at Vindolanda and at Chesters (**59**). The layouts at the two sites are similar, but the baths at Chesters are better preserved and more complex. They lie down the slope from the fort towards the river Tyne, in a spot well sited for bringing water which will have entered the fort at one of the gateways. The baths were first excavated in 1884, and appear to have had a complex history, not all of which can still be told with any confidence, partly due to the piecemeal nature of its excavation and the fact that its remains have been exposed to view for more than a century.

60 *Plan of the baths at Chesters.*

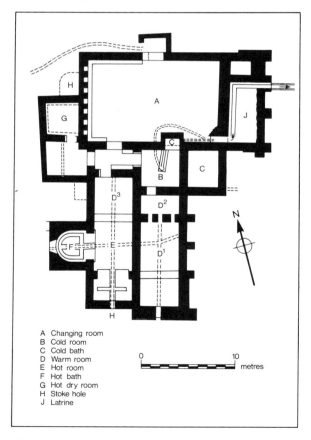

A Changing room
B Cold room
C Cold bath
D Warm room
E Hot room
F Hot bath
G Hot dry room
H Stoke hole
J Latrine

0   10
metres

The Roman bather entered the bathhouse through a small porch and entered straight-away into a large, probably fairly lofty room (**60**). This room, relatively warm from the heat of the baths, was a communal area for leisure activities of all kinds: at the end towards the river was a latrine kept constantly flushed with water flowing out of the baths. The main hall also functioned as a changing room. At one end, a row of seven niches, probably originally for a series of statues of the gods of the days of the week, are a prominent feature. The bather would slip on a pair of sandals to protect his feet from the heat of the floors suspended above hot-air ducts in the rest of the building and choose one of three treatments in the business end of the baths. Immediately to his right from the small lobby, was a dry heat treatment room; both walls and floor here were hollow and could be heated by charcoal furnaces to very high temperatures, producing a treatment something like a sauna. Relief was gained by dashing out across the lobby into the cold plunge opposite. Alternatively there lay before the bather two ranges of warm and hot rooms with interconnecting doorways, the levels of heat building up until at the far end, the pores fully open, a warm bath afforded a full relaxation (**61**). Doubtless a series of massage and cleansing treatments were also available in these suites of rooms. The loss of the floor levels in most of the rooms in the Chesters bathhouse makes it difficult to understand quite how the building functioned, but it is clear that three separate furnaces were necessary, to keep it going to full capacity, and the consumption of fuel must have been enormous. Part of the soldiers' duties — perhaps as fatigues — involved work at the baths: doubtless this included the messy jobs of cleaning them out, and keeping the furnaces stoked and in working order.

The remainder of the settlement surrounding the fort at Chesters has not been excavated, though aerial photographs show traces of buildings round its southern fringes. Survey and excavation has located elements of buildings at several other Wall forts, and some elements of the *vicus* settlements are still visible. Roman religious observances were important, and as well as the whole panoply of official gods — Jupiter, Mercury and others — who were naturally bound up with the devotional and loyal aspects of service, a spectrum of other religious cults attended the Roman

army on the Wall. Often these are known only by inscriptions on altars, some of them barely literate, set up in fulfilment of a vow.

Native gods, spirits of the countryside, or local deities of streams, with names such as Cocidius, Belatucadrus, or Mogons have dedications in Roman style at various sites, while outside Benwell fort, in a tiny temple sacred to the local god Antenociticus (see **3**, p. 00), high-ranking officers dedicated altars. Nothing is known of the god, or what he stood for. What survives is the head of his statue with its pinched features, its bold staring eyes, and its shock of hair (**62**). Just west of the fort of Carrawburgh, too, lay the well which was part of the shrine of the nymph of the stream, Coventina. Found within the well were ten altars to the goddess, dedicated by troops and their commanders from at least three different units (**63**), as well as a great variety of votive objects of all kinds, including not only coins, of which there were possibly around 16,000 in all, but also a wide variety of jewellery, in silver and bronze, as well as glass

61 *The warm rooms at Chesters bathhouse, from the south. The two openings at the near end of the baths are stoke-holes for the parallel suites of rooms, and the platform of masonry to the left of the picture at this end of the building may have been for the water tank. Floor levels in the baths were roughly at the level of the top of the central spine-wall, and all floors were suspended above heated ducts.*

vessels and other more workaday objects.

The Roman army appears in particular to have been a fertile ground for waves of new oriental cults of mystery and rebirth which swept through the empire from the second century onwards. Perhaps the most compelling of these was the cult of Mithras. The worship of the Irano-Indian god Mithras or Mithra seems to have spread from the east to Rome during the course of the first century AD, but it gained in popularity in the following centuries. As with many others of the cults which found favour at Rome, his worship became linked with

62 *The head of Antenociticus, the Celtic-style sculpture found at the temple at Benwell where altars dedicated to the god were also unearthed. This may have been part of a life-sized cult statue within the small temple (3).*

burgh Mithraeum is a narrow, stone building, the largest of a number of small temples which occupied the same site and were rebuilt time after time during the second to fourth centuries. Because of the waterlogged conditions of the ground nearby, for Coventina's Well and spring is not far away, elements of timber were well preserved at the time of its excavation in 1949–50. Since Roman timber does not long survive exposure to the air, these have been replaced in concrete so that in all respects the temple can now be seen in the form it was discovered by its excavators.

63 *The water-goddess Coventina reclines on a water-lily leaf, while holding a water-plant as a sceptre, and her spring emerges from the jar on which her elbow rests. One of the sculptures found within a well, evidently dedicated to the goddess, at Carrawburgh.*

that of other Roman deities. Mithras however appears to have been in origin a sun-god who was born from heaven, and whose act of creation was to capture a white bull, take it to his cave and sacrifice it; from the blood which poured out all manner of other creatures gained new life. This doctrine of new life through sacrifice is one which brought Mithraism into close conflict with Christianity.

Mithraic temples are known from three of the settlements surrounding Hadrian's Wall forts, Housesteads, Rudchester and Carrawburgh, but it is only at the latter that the remains can still be seen (64). The god's temples are small, confined spaces, supposed to represent the cave in which the bull-slaying episode took place. The number of devotees was therefore necessarily limited, and inscriptions from elsewhere reveal that the brotherhood was rather like a secret society, with levels of initiation to undergo, all of it conducted in secret. Carraw-

The temple lay roughly north-west to south-east, with a doorway at its southern end. The first quarter of the buildings' length was taken up with an entrance lobby, screened from the remainder of the temple by a wooden partition. Here was a small statue of a mother goddess. The central portion of the temple was a narrow central aisle flanked by Mithras' two torch-bearing attendants with low benches on either side, leaving the far end of the temple free for the cult ceremonies (**65**). A shelf on the end wall was probably intended as a support for a large picture or sculpture of Mithras slaying the bull — similar scenes are known from other sites — and in front of it stood three altars. It is clear that drama formed part of the ceremonial: one of the altars has a series of pierced holes forming Mithras' crown, and the light from a torch set in the recess behind this would have provided a dramatic moment in the ritual. The arrangement of wooden posts supporting the roof is complex at the 'business end' of the temple, and it is not impossible that this was to provide a higher temple roof over this portion, in contrast to the low, cavern-like nave. It would have been possible by drawing a curtain in this

64 *Carrawburgh mithraeum stands in a low, sometimes waterlogged site just outside the south-west corner of the fort. Several mithraic temples occupied this site from the second century onwards, and none was very large. The outer walls of this one, the latest and biggest, were of stone, but much of the internal arrangements were of wood which was found on excavation to have survived well. The altars and the 'wooden remains' seen on the site today, however, are casts of what was originally found.*

high portion of the building to allow sunlight to stream in, thus illuminating the backdrop of Mithras slaying the bull, the triumph of light over darkness.

Nowhere better than at Vindolanda does one gain the impression of a sprawling clutter of buildings assembled round one of the main roads leading to the gate (**66**). Excavators there have revealed that there were two main layouts of the *vicus* belonging to forts of different phases. The first appears to have belonged with the Hadrianic fort, and to have been set within a clay rampart for added protection. It incorpor-

65 *Reconstructed impression of the innermost portion of Carrawburgh mithraeum. Mithras' two attendants, holding torches aloft and shielded to signify light and darkness respectively, flank the narrow aisle. Benches lie to left and right for worshippers and initiates, and the cult area lies before the altars at the temple's far end.*

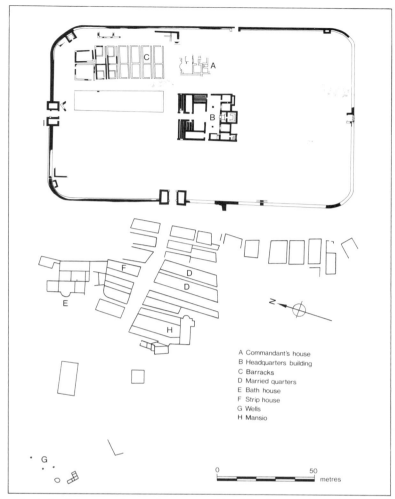

A Commandant's house
B Headquarters building
C Barracks
D Married quarters
E Bath house
F Strip house
G Wells
H Mansio

0   50
                          metres

ated not only the fort bathhouse, but also a substantial official lodging house or hotel, with a central corridor with rooms off it, and its own small suite of baths. Other buildings, partially obscured by elements of the later *vicus* which lie above them, seem to have been long narrow near-rectangular shops or houses normally fronting onto the main street. Towards the end of the second century and at the beginning of the third — at just about the time that round huts appeared within the fort (see p. 102) — the *vicus* seems to have been abandoned, but it grew up again to substantial size during the course of the third century. This time it covered a greater area, and incorporated not only the baths and the former hotel, but also a number of other shops, workshops or domestic buildings which have produced evidence for various industrial processes — including bronze work-

66 *The fort and settlement at Vindolanda. This plan shows the buildings now visible on the site which formed part of the later of the two phases of settlement at the site. It includes a bath-house and a* mansio, *an official rest-house for the imperial messenger system.*

ing, weaving and spinning, lime burning and the manufacture of objects out of shale. Sufficient evidence existed to suggest to excavators that pottery was being made nearby and that milling and the tanning of leather goods was being carried out locally.

Inscriptions and other finds from many other Wall sites add more detail about the quality of life in such settlements. Inscriptions set up by villagers are normally either tombstones or religious dedications. The placing of an inscription on a tomb to record the death of a loved

67 *The tombstone of Regina from South Shields. This elaborately sculpted stone marks the last resting place of Regina, the British wife of a man named Barates, probably a merchant, from Palmyra. The dead woman sits on a wicker chair, in an arched pediment which is typical of eastern funerary sculpture: the stone may therefore have been carved by a craftsman from the east.*

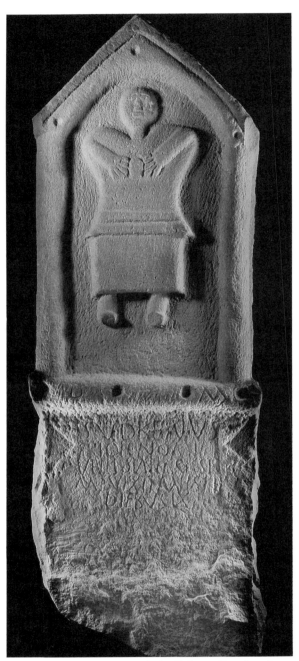

68 *The tombstone of Vellibia Ertola from Corbridge. In complete contrast to the stone of Regina from South Shields (67), this little girl's gravestone is crudely carved, barely literate, but with a conventional Roman figure of a little child clutching a ball, in what is almost a pastiche of what four-year-old Vellibia might have drawn herself.*

wife, husband, child or parent was a final Roman act of piety which appears to have been done by rich and relatively poor alike: a rich merchant like Barathes from Syria could set up a very elaborate memorial at South Shields to his British wife and freedwoman Regina who died at the age of thirty (**67**). Others are barely literate — like the tombstone of Vellibia Ertola which shows the little girl, just over four years old when she died, clutching a ball in front of her in both hands (**68**). No cemetery associated with a Hadrian's Wall fort has been excavated, but the examination of the remains of the inhabitants of the Wall and its associated settlements in a comprehensive fashion would give some very revealing glimpses of the conditions of life in the frontier zone. Quite apart from showing the mix of population in the area — the relative numbers of men, women and children, something of their racial types, their nutritional state, diseases to which they were prone or had suffered, the wear and tear which life had inflicted on their bodies — the study of a cemetery would also show what their average life expectancy was. If it was anything like the cemeteries examined in the poorer quarters of York or elsewhere, this would show that women might be lucky to live to the age of thirty, and men to about forty, though of course there were considerable exceptions to this.

By no means all the population would consider a tombstone necessary, and it is therefore likely that those tombstones which do survive were either military ones — perhaps paid for by the soldiers' insurance payments to the 'burial club' — or of people who had a particular predilection to Roman forces of ceremony. The same must also be true of religious dedications: those who dedicated altars to Roman gods, or local gods accepted into the seemingly limitless

69 *Plan of the central part of the town at Corbridge. The series of forts (9) lay deeply buried beneath this late second or early third century layout. Only the store buildings occupied the same site in the fort and town. Next to the granaries lies the aqueduct (see 71), and the forum; to the south of the road through the middle of the site (which is actually the Stanegate) parts of the two walled compounds can be made out. The building identified as the headquarters or administrative block in each of them is marked as 'HQ'. Sites of probable temples (see 73) are marked 'T'.*

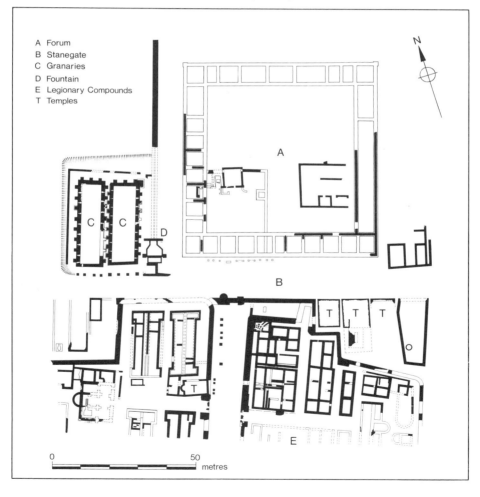

A Forum
B Stanegate
C Granaries
D Fountain
E Legionary Compounds
T Temples

0   50
                 metres

Roman pantheon, did so in a peculiarly traditional way, perhaps in fulfilment of a promise made to the god when invoking help for a particular crisis, such as a journey, a successful birth, or safe return from a military campaign. We do not know what a non-Roman expression of worship to such local deities might have been.

This leads inescapably to one of the major problems for the archaeologist in this Roman frontier land. Who lived in the *vici* round the forts? If they were people collected from the

70 *These buttressed stores at Corbridge were built in the latter part of the second century on the site of similar buildings which had belonged to the military forts. They have loading platforms at the far end towards the street, and these frontages were furnished with four columns, perhaps to support a portico, which may even have allowed loading of stores to an upper level. The eastern (left-hand) building was almost certainly double storeyed; both of them retain a good deal of their flagged floors suspended above ventilation flues.*

surrounding areas, the former native farmers or their children, quick to latch on to the commercial opportunities which opened up from the presence of the military, one may ask why there is so little sign of depopulation in the frontier areas. It does not seem so satisfactory to postulate that they came from the rather more romanised south, following the army through the country and settling at the gates of any available fort, although it is clearly not impossible that this should have happened. Either way, our evidence is one-sided and weighted towards the Roman side of the argument. Those who dedicated tombstones, raised altars to Romanised gods, or used Roman artefacts have left ample evidence. If there was a native undercurrent it cannot so easily be recognised, and we are left with the difficulty of reconciling two kinds of evidence for civilians in the north. One shows people still living in the Roman period in a pre-Roman agricultural based farming system, largely independent of Rome's influence, while the other shows the lifestyle of people in the settlements round the forts, who have accepted their de-

pendence on the military presence and who have espoused many of Rome's outward forms of material culture and styles of life.

The two most substantial settlements in the Wall region, both of which owed their origins to the collections of civilian buildings round early forts, are Carlisle and Corbridge. A fort at Carlisle was established probably by Agricola in the AD 80s, and a settlement will probably have been attracted round its southern fringes. Excavation oppotunities in the city of Carlisle have been limited, but it is clear that there were substantial stone buildings, including a number of town houses, within the urban area. It is probable that the walled medieval city has taken its shape from a similar Roman pattern but the presence of Roman defences has not been confirmed.

The presence of a modern city on top of its medieval and Roman predecessors has made the examination of the Roman occupation of Carlisle a complex and rather piecemeal problem, but the other major Roman settlement near the Wall has presented no such difficulties. The site of Corbridge lies about half a mile west of the centre of the modern village, and owes its position to the establishment on this spot of a fort, around AD 85, to guard the crossing-point of the River Tyne. A succession of forts occupied the terrace above the north bank of the river until about the 160s, when, with the final abandonment of the Antonine frontier in Scotland, there seems to have been a complete change in attitude to the fort site. The main street across the fort from east to west was retained, but its ramparts appear to have been levelled, and most of its buildings demolished. In its place a rather more expansive layout was begun (69). North of the road, the fort granaries were rebuilt in rather more massive style (70): these are still today the most imposing buildings on the site, even though they survive only up to Roman raised floor levels. Next to them an elaborate aqueduct and fountain, constructed by legionary builders from the twentieth legion (71–2), and, on a freshly levelled site which incorporated the site of much of the headquarters, commandant's house and parts of the barracks of the earlier fort, was a large courtyard building covering nearly an acre. This appears to have been intended as the market place if not the forum for a new planned town to take the place of the fort. Excavations revealed, however, that this ambitious layout

71 *The Corbridge aqueduct. Water was brought into the site from the north along an enclosed channel which was supported, at least in its last stretch, on an embankment. At its culmination, a fountain was provided to supply running water for the town, and an elaborate series of tanks and conduits fed the supply to many different quarters. Beyond the aqueduct's remains can be seen a portion of the uncompleted forum or market-place.*

hardly progressed beyond the foundation stage before the project, at least in this spacious form, was abandoned. No trace of a basilica to go with the 'forum' can be found, and there is no obvious sign of any further layout of a town into *insulae*, regular islands of development, such as is indicative of planned towns further south.

South of the main road through the site, a

72 *Artist's view of the Corbridge aqueduct: The basin and water-tanks and the bases for the statues exist on the site, and the pediment sculpture is in the site museum.*

73 *Reconstructed view of the Corbridge temples, looking at the buildings which flank the south side of the Stanegate. These small rectangular buildings have actually left few clues as to their original purpose, but the fact that the compound walls were carefully planned so as to avoid them suggests that they had an established claim on the street frontages. This drawing shows the narrow gateway from the east compound which gives onto the Stanegate.*

number of rather less regular developments had been taking place; small properties fronted onto the main street. One was a pottery shop or warehouse, others may have been temples (**73**). For some reason, control was lost over the process of developing this part of the site, for, slightly later, when further buildings were added, they had to occupy space tucked in behind these existing frontages. These new buildings comprised two quarters of semi-military nature, each with what appears to have been a small administrative block: besides this the western one contains long narrow buildings which may have been workshops, but could

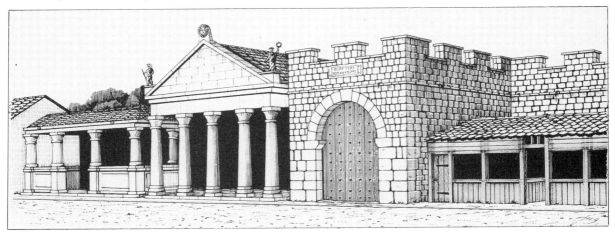

have served many different purposes, while the eastern one contained a pair of substantial houses as well as a number of smaller buildings of unknown function. Both these groups of buildings would be less remarkable were it not for the fact that each was surrounded by a substantial wall, snaking round in existing spaces between buildings left inside or outside their protective ring. The enclosure walls contained main gateways which faced each other across a side street, thus suggesting that the two compounds were related, and that they were of military purpose. Inscribed stones and other evidence from Corbridge shows that two legions, the twentieth and the sixth, were active at the site, and it has been suggested therefore that the compounds were the bases for the stationing of detachments of legionary troops assigned to outpost duties from their main body. Thus Corbridge can be seen as a part-garrison town in the Wall zone.

The site is an enormously complex one, little helped by the fact that what is today on view

74 *Aerial view of the site at Corbridge. The pattern of streets of the Roman town shows clearly as parched marks in the field around the central portion of the site where the remains are open to view. Close inspection reveals the traces of several large buildings lining the streets.*

in only the central portion of a far larger, possibly walled, urban sprawl. It is a fort-settlement writ larger, which has expanded to take over and obliterate the site of its parent fort. Aerial photography shows the extent of buildings which still exist, many of them totally unexplored, outside the central area (**74**): this shows well the rather haphazard and unplanned nature of the township. Combined with evidence from earlier excavations, carried out in 1906–14, which exposed traces of buildings which have not been re-examined since, the town is clearly centred round the compounds and the unfinished forum, but contained a good many other buildings which would not have been out of place in any of the civilian settlements round forts on the line of the Wall. Even at Corbridge, however, where much of the excavation of buildings belonging to the town took place prior to the First World War without all the benefits of modern excavation techniques, it is not possible to determine a great deal about the history of the site in the third and fourth centuries.

What is evident, however, from the finds from the earliest as from more recent excavations at the site, is the quality of much of the building. Many highly crafted sculptured stones have been found at the site. One of the best known, the Corbridge lion — in origin probably a tombstone, with a favourite motif of the lion devouring its prey — was found re-used as a fountain in one of the substantial houses on the terrace overlooking the river (**colour plate 4**). Other sculptured stones, mainly of religious character, are of startling quality: from a number of temples now no longer identifiable come statues of gods, goddesses and other whose significance cannot now be guessed at: prime among these is a series of sculptures which once adorned a temple to Jupiter Dolichenus, another of the eastern mystery cults which, like Mithraism, came to prominence in the second and third centuries. These include an altar to the god, linked with Brigantia, who must have been a local deity associated with the Brigantes themselves, as well as portions of the temple pediment and other cult statues which show that the temple was of some sophistication (**colour plate 5**).

Elsewhere in southern Britain, as Roman troops moved out and moved on, towns which ultimately gained self-governing status took their place. On the Wall it is not clear to what extent the civilian communities achieved any sort of similar independence. The only indications come from inscriptions: of the four examples which mention village-dwellers (*vicani*) in the settlements round forts in north Britain, it is clear from two of them that not only was concerted 'village' action possible, but also that there was probably a measure of self-government in the existence of a 'council', and the passing of resolutions, as well as the collection of public subscriptions. Such village councils however may have been little more than a substratum of official control tolerated by military commanders on the understanding that it would help to enforce their own jurisdiction, ease the collection of taxes due or otherwise enforce discipline in the proximity of serving troops. Such settlements clustered round the gates of the forts could never really expect to be self-supporting or politically independent.

Carlisle and Corbridge, however, are in a different category, and there is some evidence to suggest both that the name *Luguvallium* and the status as capital of a tribal unit (of the Carvetii) had been assigned to Carlisle by the latter part of the second century. Corbridge is a different matter, for not only is the traditional name Corstopitum now seen to be corrupt (its Roman name was more likely to have been something like *Corielsopitum*), but there is also no evidence whatsoever for its urban status.

Such evidence as there is points to a growing interdependence of forts and their *vici*. By the fourth century, the defensible fort might therefore be seen as a natural refuge for civilians clustering round it in times of danger. From this it is but a relatively short step to suggest that the forts themselves may eventually have housed civilians — at least the wives and families of soldiers — at some point in the fourth or even fifth century. The civilian population, perhaps a mixture of locals, merchants, families and followers, was always at hand and had a positive contribution to make to the Roman military patterns of life in the frontier zone.

8

The static frontier

The peace purchased by Severus' governor Virius Lupus on the northern frontier in the late 190s seems to have been a precarious one. A number of inscriptions from northern forts, not all of them on Hadrian's Wall, record rebuilding in the early years of the third century. One

75 *Risingham fort from the air. The outline of the fort shows dramatically in this view: its ramparts and gates are particularly well visible. Most of the prominent earthworks within the fort, however, are of post-Roman date: the Roman layout lies buried at a deeper level.*

76 *The written rock of Gelt: inscription on a Roman quarry near Brampton, Cumbria. A number of inscriptions were left by Roman soldiers while working at the quarry face (not necessarily at the same time); this one records the consuls Aper and Maximus (the date AD 207) and the Oficina Mercati, or 'Mercatus' yard'.*

of them is the outpost fort at Risingham on the road leading northwards from Corbridge, where the 1000-strong cohort of Vangiones 'rebuilt the walls and gate which had fallen down because they were so old' (**75**). Storehouses were built at Corbridge and at Birdoswald, and a very precise inscription on the Roman quarry face near Brampton records that in 207, when

77 *The circular buildings in the fort at Vindolanda. Traces of three rows, each of five huts, have been found in the north-east corner of the fort. They have for long puzzled archaeologists, and nothing like them has been found elsewhere within a Roman fort. They were probably special accommodation provided for some reason within the fort, but the circumstances are unknown.*

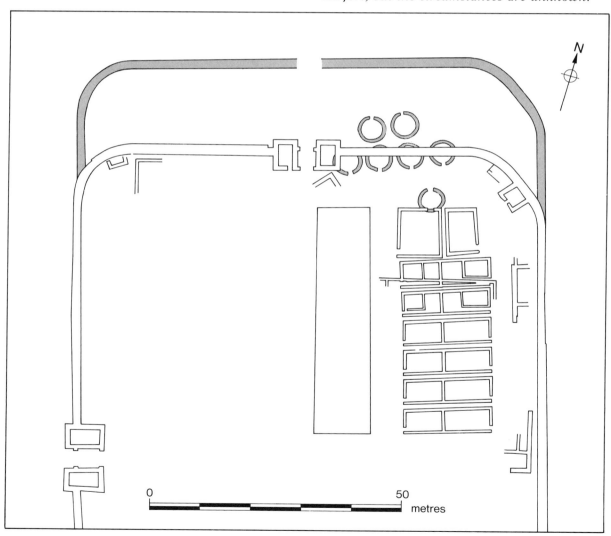

Aper and Maximus were consuls, Mercatus' yard was in the business of extracting stone (76). Whether Mercatus was a military officer or a civilian contractor supplying army needs is not known.

One of the most unusual developments in any Roman fort to date can be assigned to this period at Vindolanda. The first stone fort at Vindolanda was established under Hadrian: to its west lay the flourishing settlement which it attracted. Tucked into the fort's north-east corner, however, excavators have long been puzzled by a series of rows of circular buildings, quite unlike anything ever encountered within a Roman fort before (77). They were later than other, more regular structures, and formed at least three regular rows of round huts occupying the sort of space one would normally expect to be occupied by barrack blocks within the second-century fort. The best explanation of these is that they formed special accommodation within the fort for civilians or other inhabitants who would be better located within round separate huts than in separate rooms within a barrack. They could have been intended for parties of civilian builders working on the forts and on the rebuilding of the wall, for several undated inscriptions recording civilian working-parties on the Wall have been found (78). They could equally well have been special provision for prisoners of war.

That there was military action as well as rebuilding in the military zone at this time seems certain. Dedications of altars to the emperors' victory — one of them apparently suggesting that it was the Brigantes who had been defeated — reflect the tense situation in AD 207–8, but may record nothing more serious than small skirmishes. The situation rapidly deteriorated, however, to the point where the governor of Britain considered that stronger action was required and reported on the state of affairs to the emperor. Severus, anxious to give his sons a taste of active service and to drag them away from what he regarded as their life of idleness in Rome, needed little persuasion to lead an expeditionary force: it set out in 208. Commemorative coins were struck, and troops for the campaign in Britain were gathered from several continental legions. Despite Severus' own disabilities — he had to be carried in a litter because of his arthritis — the collected force made good speed to Britain, and several inscriptions from mainland Europe as well as

78 *Inscriptions left by British civilians working on the Wall. Stones such as these are common along the line of the Wall, and most of them record sections of Wall construction undertaken by units of troops under this or that commanding officer. These record building — perhaps forced labour — undertaken by the Civitas Dumnoniorum (from Exeter), and by the Civitas Catuvellaunarum (from St Albans).*

the legends on coins commemorate the commitment to this British expeditionary force.

The actual campaigns began in earnest in 209. Coins which portray galleys on their reverse suggest that the advance was by sea as well as land, but the accounts of the campaign in the works of the historians Dio Cassius and Herodian seek to lay stress on the difficulty of the terrain through which the advancing army had to force its way. They record that on Severus' arrival the Britons sued for peace, but Severus had decided on a punitive expedition and was not to be put off. He left his younger son Geta in charge of affairs in the Roman part of the province and prepared for the push northwards. His force crossed the Wall, but found it hard to get the Caledonians to give battle in the approved Roman manner. A guerrilla campaign ensued, with false trails being laid, and Roman soldiers lured to their deaths in swamps and marshes: Dio relates that 50,000 Romans were killed, a figure which is scarcely credible but, if true, would have been disastrous.

Indications from archaeological remains tell a rather more positive story of Roman achievements. A fort at Carpow on the south bank of the River Tay was provided for a legionary detachment of the sixth and second legions, and a further fort was established at Cramond on the Firth of Forth. Additional evidence of the extent of the campaigns is provided by a number of marching-camps — temporary accommodation for elements of the expeditionary force — which have been assigned to this phase of the various Roman contacts with Scotland. The dating of temporary camps of this nature, which may have contained only tents or other makeshift accommodation, is always a problem, unless chance finds afford for the archaeologist a group of typical pottery or other debris which can help establish a date. Camps usually assigned to this period, however, contain space for a number of separate detachments of different sizes. The pattern their discovery has revealed, which is that of a number of camps which have the same internal area, suggests the slow, steady progress northwards of the Roman force in separate units, and corresponds quite closely with the accounts of the campaigns left by the historians. If all the camps are correctly assigned to this date, and the arguments rely mainly on the sequence of temporary camps of several different campaigns at particularly favoured 'launching pad' sites like Ardoch, they show that penetration into Scotland by the Severan armies was at least as deep, if not as effective, as that achieved by Agricola about 130 years earlier. The expedition arrived in some strength at the Firth of Forth, and then spread via a number of different routes up to the fringes of the Highland Zone, as Agricola's line of forts had earlier done, and up into the area west of Aberdeen.

The historians' accounts of the campaigns do not make it at all clear what was actually achieved. If Severus' aim was a punitive expedition, success was probably at best only partial. There was relative peace, however, for many years after the beginning of the third century. If his aim had been the reoccupation of Scotland, it was accompanied by surprisingly little progress towards establishing the network of permanent posts which would have been required to hold the territory. An achievement of some sort in Britain was celebrated in 210 by Severus' assumption of the title *Britannicus*, perhaps with the conclusion of a successful peace-treaty which ceded control of some at least of lowland Scotland to the Romans. There are signs that further campaigns were in preparation in 211 when Severus died in York. Caracalla and Geta became joint emperors, at

least in name, and their attention turned from military affairs in northern Britain to the question of which of them was to occupy the throne on his own.

One of the sites most often seen as associated with the campaigns of Severus is the fort at the mouth of the Tyne at South Shields. Here, at a prominent position on its southern bank and near a bend in the river which afforded a reasonable harbour, Roman occupation is attested from the time of Agricola onwards. Timber buildings which may have belonged to a fort, or to a succession of them, as at Corbridge, underlie the first stone fort built in 163 which probably had sufficient accommodation for a mixed cohort of 500 men. Developments at the site, probably in the early third century, but not yet precisely datable, were startling: the fort was extended southwards by as much as a half as much again of its original area and virtually the entire area which had been the extent of the original fort was covered by a series of twenty new granary buildings (**79**). Not only this but in addition the fort headquarters itself was converted into a pair of granaries, and the original granary buildings belonging to the earlier fort were retained — a total of twenty-four such buildings in all. The fort was converted into a massive supply base, with accommodation for its garrison squeezed into a small newly-built extension.

Whether this major provision of storage space was primarily a support for Severus' campaigns into Scotland cannot be determined for certain. If so, the store-buildings themselves evidently had a longer life than this, for many of them seem to have been retained in use until well into the third or fourth centuries. The extended southern part of the site now contained the rather cramped barrack accommodation for its garrison and included a small headquarters building. At a later stage, probably towards the end of the third century, much of this layout in the southern part of the fort was devastated by fire, and new accommodation for troops erected. This, surprisingly, consisted of the conversion of eight of the former granaries back into barracks, by subdividing them into *contubernia* for the men, and their extension at one end to provide accommodation for their commanding officers. More barracks of similar type, but newly built, were also erected in the southern part of the site (**80**). In the meanwhile the larger original headquarters had

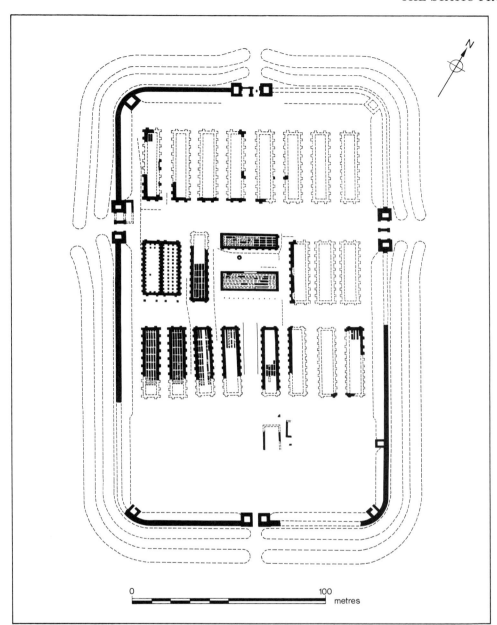

79 *Plan of South Shields fort in the later second or early third century. Most of the northern part of the site is covered with a series of store buildings, leaving the extended southern portion the only space available for accommodation for the garrison.*

been rebuilt, to face south, and was thus accessible from the side where the accommodation for the men lay. A wall was built to separate the storage area of the site from the barracks.

Not all of these developments can yet be closely dated, but the continued emphasis on

South Shields as a stores-base in the third century and beyond suggests that the supply of foodstuffs and other materials to troops on frontier duty was being carefully planned. A sample of grain from the site has been analysed and can be shown to contain species which are

80 *Barrack-blocks in South Shields fort, as revealed by recent excavation. Part of a courtyard house lies to the left, and portions of the barrack rooms to the right. Each of the separate units within the barrack seems to have been divided into two, a front and a back room, approached through a narrow linking corridor. There were cobbled floors and internal partitions of wood, wattle and daub.*

more likely to have come from the continent than Britain. There are references to grain being sent from the Rhineland to Britain in historical sources, but not as early as the third century. If this provision was necessary from around AD 200 onwards, questions arise about the arrangements which had been made earlier for the supply of the necessary foodstuffs and equipment for the considerable numbers of men in garrison on the Wall. It may be that sites such as that discovered and partly excavated at Walton-le-Dale near Preston provide at least part of the answer for the Hadrianic period and the second century.

Severus' presence in Britain clearly gave a great fillip to Roman considerations about the frontier. Several late Roman historical sources — perhaps drawing on the same original source material — credited Severus with the construction of the Wall, and the extent of his rebuilding or recommissioning of parts of the wall-system may have been considerable. Rationalisation of the provision of turrets, sometimes involving their suppression and dismantling, may have been carried out now rather than earlier (p. 75), and there is evidence that some sections of the Wall required fundamental rebuilding or repair. Portions of this may not even have been built above foundation level in the first place. One of the most striking examples of a rebuilt stretch of Wall is in the area east of milecastle 39, where the Wall rises up to Hotbank crags. Here the narrow gauge Wall built round a core of rubble bound with mortar of great solidity, rises off the broad foundation. This may have originally supported a Wall of intermediate gauge.

Milecastles came in for some replanning now. The provision of gateways was reviewed, and some — for example the north gate of milecastle 37 — were reduced in width to make them passable on foot only. Other changes, possibly brought about because of the collapse of gate-towers, seem to have been more fundamental, and involved the substitution of new gate-jambs and lintels rather than rebuilding of their arches. Internally, too, there was some alteration to the layout in those that have been examined. It is probable that the pair of neatly opposed 'barracks' at Poltross Burn milecastle (no 48) were brought into commission now, replacing an earlier, as yet undiscovered arrangement, but these buildings seem scarcely

81 *The developing plan of Sewingshields milecastle. (A) the Hadrianic phase; (B) early third century; (C) late third century; (D) fourth century. Many of the later changes were represented by re-planning of the internal partitions in the building on the west side of the enclosure.*

typical of the far more untidy dispositions discovered at other, more recently excavated, examples.

At Sewingshields (81) the internal arrangements in the third and fourth centuries are complex: buildings were planned on both sides of the central road. Traces of them recovered in excavation were fragmentary, but they appear to have filled both portions of the available internal space. The south gateway was partially blocked, and a well-laid path led up to the western of the two buildings, which was divided internally into at least two rooms. Outside the milecastle wall, in the angle between the east wall and Hadrian's Wall there was a hearth, suggesting that occupation of the milecastles spilled out beyond the internal area. At Castle Nick milecastle (no 39), a similar pattern seems to have been followed, although the dating of the phases is as yet unclear. Following the establishment of the first stone phase of milecastle buildings — a three-roomed barrack — rebuilding took place, with a series of buildings with small curving porches covering part of the surface of the central road.

More evidence for rebuilding at various times in the third century comes from many of the forts in the northern zone in the form of inscriptions rather than the archaeological remains. A number of these, like that at Risingham (see 75, pp. 101–2), mention portions of forts built or rebuilt now 'because older buildings had fallen down' or 'because a violent fire had destroyed the earlier ones'. These have sometimes been seen as veiled references to the destruction of fort buildings by hostile action — the very awkwardness of the explanation for rebuilding interpreted as a sure sign that there is something to cover up. This is not altogether satisfactory, however, and reads too much into the rather pompous honorific inscriptions of the time. What seems hard to understand, if these statements are to be taken at face value, is why so many fort buildings were in such a bad state. To take only those on Hadrian's Wall itself, a granary at Greatchesters was restored in 225, and at Birdoswald, the commandant's house was restored between 296–305. Elsewhere, in forts in northern Britain, the same formula is used to record rebuilding on aqueducts, bath-houses, basilicas, temples and, in one case at Lanchester, the headquarters building and armoury. The circumstances which had led to this apparent neglect of building maintenance

on the part of the occupying garrison lead to further speculation about the distribution of troop garrisons or at least about the levels of morale in the Roman army of the third century.

Archaeological developments belonging to the third century are not easy to identify. Inscriptions from many of the Wall forts suggest that several of the fort-garrisons changed yet again: the only one known to have remained unchanged from the late second century is the *Ala II Asturum* which was in occupation at Chesters. By and large, however, units once established on the Wall in the early third century seem to have stayed put for a considerable time, probably for 150 years or more. A late Roman document listing all the civil and military postings in the Roman world at the end of the fourth century includes a list of the Hadrian's Wall forts: virtually all of them, where this can be checked, are recorded as then having the same units in occupation as are attested on surviving inscriptions of the third century. Certain fixed points can be seized on: at Vindolanda, an inscription reads that a gate with its towers was rebuilt from the foundations in AD 223–5. This seems to have been the west gate, leading to the *vicus*, and its rebuilding was accompanied by re-planning of part of the fort's circuit walls. Excavations within the fort have revealed that stone-built barracks were soon constructed within the newly rearranged fort. These were unlike the barracks of earlier forts — a number of linked buildings, subdivided into separate rooms for the men, with accommodation for their officers at one end. The buildings, however, are separate units rather than long barracks subdivided into individual rooms.

Considerable alterations also took place to at least two of the Wall bridges, perhaps in the wake of severe floods which swept away the Hadrianic bridges at Willowford and Chesters. At Willowford, repairs seem to have been of a more makeshift nature. The replacement of the original bridge in wood had taken place in the middle of the second century, and the third rebuilding involved the provision of flood channels to ease the pressure on the structure from the river when it was in spate as well as a general widening of the bridge which would have enabled it to accommodate a roadway. A similar, though possibly more impressive, development took place at Chesters. Most of the visible remains of the large eastern abutment (see **23**, p. 37) belong to the bridge reconstructed in the early decades of the third century. It was stone-built, and crossed the river in three substantial piers, rather than the eight of the earlier Hadrianic bridge (see **24**, p. 38; **colour plate 7**). Close study of the wealth of carved stone from the site suggests that it was an elegant structure, all of stone. It carried a roadway between parapets of narrow stone slabs slotted into place in grooves in the bridge structure. Four large stone columns formed a decorative element and marked the beginning and end of the bridge; similar pillars are known from other sites, but those at Chesters (one can still be seen lying on the remains of the abutment) bear no dedicatory inscription. Standing on the east abutment was a tower, the base of the gatehouse leading to the bridge, and an earth ramp will have carried the roadway up to it. Within the tower, a hearth produced an archaeomagnetic date of around AD 220. There is no sign of later rebuilding of the bridge at Chesters, but at a later date the southern part of the new abutment was extended, and a water channel was built across the abutment through the base of the tower. This probably served a mill downstream from the bridge.

There are substantial difficulties in equating the archaeological record of what was happening to installations on Hadrian's Wall in the third and fourth centuries with the historical texts, among them the inscriptions which record rebuilding after a period of neglect. Excavators at Haltonchesters and at Rudchester have been able to point to elements of buildings within the forts there which appear to have been rebuilt only after a long gap in occupation which had allowed layers of soil or debris to build up over collapsed remains of buildings. This does not square well, however, with the other evidence which suggests continuity of occupation of the forts by a permanent garrison. In few cases, however, have excavations been comprehensive enough to give a clear sequence of the shifts in occupation within a single fort throughout this period. One site, Wallsend, where relatively comprehensive excavations have taken place, has shown that some areas of the central part of the fort were always left clear of buildings, while others, including some of the early streets, became cluttered in later periods with permanent or temporary buildings. In the northern part of the site, some of the barrack buildings were left — possibly

in decay — while others were remodelled in startlingly different fashion (**82**). Excavation at any one of these particular spots within the fort rather than the more comprehensive campaign of exploration which has been possible might have come up with any number of varying stories about abandonment or continuity: only by looking at the total picture of the fort's occupation can one hope to clarify the picture.

That there were substantial changes in the accommodation provided within forts is becoming very clear indeed, though there is no general rule about this. Many of the central buildings, the headquarters, storebuildings and the commandants' houses, remained part of the standard plan: small modifications, for example the provision of a latrine in the headquarters at Vindolanda, or the addition of a luxurious bath-suite and the conversion of many of the rooms in the Chesters commandant's house to hypocausted accommodation, show, as should be expected, that 150 years of occupation will mean continual modifications and improvements. Changes to the barracks, however, if they could be interpreted, might show something more striking about what was happening to the garrison itself at the time. Work at Housesteads and at Wallsend has revealed in several instances that former long barrack-blocks consisting of centurion's accommodation at one end with barrack-rooms for groups of the men under his command were totally re-planned in the third and fourth centuries. Some walls from the earlier barracks were utilised to form a basis for a number of separate structures, normally detached from their fellows, with narrow passages between them. The numbers of these separate units rather like a row of beach-huts, increasingly termed 'chalets' by today's excavators, vary from place to place: in two barracks at Housesteads there are eight and six such buildings respectively. Those at Wallsend are even more irregular and oddly-shaped.

The growth of settlements of civilians around Wall forts in the third and fourth centuries has already been noted (p. 87), and the effects of new conditions of service within the Roman army introduced in the early third century, which included the right to marry legally, will have made some difference to troops like those on Hadrian's Wall on frontier postings. In time, this all led to a lack of mobility among troops stationed on a static frontier: they became unprepared for new campaigns, developed a

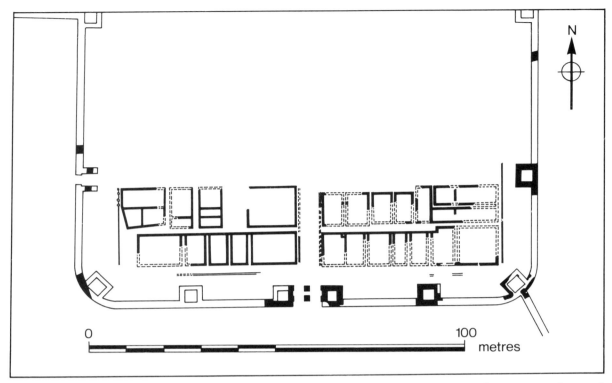

82 *Fourth-century barracks at Wallsend. These occupied the site of two of the original barracks, and differed considerably from their long, narrow, regular planning. The late Roman arrangements here were to furnish a number of separate and irregular huts or 'chalets', possibly for the individual occupancy of a soldier and his family.*

stable lifestyle, put down roots, started families and needed more private accommodation. It is indeed possible, though difficult to prove, that the 'chalets' recognised in some of the Hadrian's wall forts were accommodation for individual soldiers and their families. If so, the size of the garrison may have been cut down drastically, for in the space where up to eighty men were accommodated in Hadrianic times, there may only now have been about eight, with wives, families and children. Other men could of course have lived in the accompanying settlements — after all the inhabitants of these had to come from somewhere — but the whole process, if this is a true picture, shows potential for a laxity of discipline, the onset of lethargy and inertia, and the loss of a real taste for battle. Such trends are documented across the

rest of the Roman army in later centuries, and Britain cannot have been immune from them. Whether the 'chalets' and other developments in the forts on the Wall are actually signs of this process at work can only be decided when there is some hard evidence. This may only be imparted by the excavation of a fort, its settlement and its cemetery, to give an adequate cross-section of the changing mix of the fort and its dependent population.

Perhaps surprisingly, there is also evidence that some milecastles were continuously occupied until well into the fourth century. At Sewingshields, the internal buildings underwent a constant series of modifications in its later periods, and the finds from the site, a considerable number of which were weapons or other military equipment, spanned the whole of the fourth century. Neither here, however, nor at milecastle 39, has it so far been possible to determine the make-up of the milecastle garrison: if the suggestions above concerning the men in the forts are accurate, something similar may also have been happening in the milecastles, and they could have become home for a very small number of men indeed and their families. A corollary of the stability of military life and part of the conversion from soldier into settler might also be the commencement of farming in a limited way in the area. The milecastles could now be seen, therefore, as enclosing small farming communities, the menfolk nominally in active service, and still paid from a central authority, but actually called upon to carry out fewer demanding duties.

Emergencies did on occasion still arise, but the solution in the fourth century at least was to have available a mobile strike force, on higher pay than the frontier garrisons, who could be called upon to combat the necessary pressure. In any case, as far as Hadrian's Wall was concerned, its role as a control for access to the British province, though important, was always supplemented by the provision of intelligence about potential trouble in the area to the north of the Wall. Certain of the forts to the north of the Wall were still garrisoned: the name given to Netherby, *castra exploratorum*, suggests that scouts or intelligence officers (*exploratores*) were stationed there. The impression gained, after Severus' hectic activity in Scotland in the early years of the third century, is of a more watchful approach by the Roman forces, and one which allowed their preparedness for action, though not their hold on the Wall, to become more and more restricted. Historical sources for the fourth century mention military problems in northern Britain on several occasions. By AD 300 there is the earliest mention of the Picts, already a troublesome nation, who made their presence more and more evident during the course of the fourth century. Britain by now was only an increasing irrelevance, so far as contemporary historians were concerned, and detailed description of military doings in the island was given relatively short shrift.

Fragments of evidence make it possible to suggest that around AD 305–6 the emperor Constantius celebrated a victory over the Picts. Constans, emperor in 343, seems also to have visited Britain, and whatever he did there, made some dispositions with regard to people called the *areani*, who appear to have had some connection with the northern frontier. A few years later, in 360, the emperor Julian heard of trouble in Britain while he was wintering at Paris. The Picts (from Scotland) and Scots (from Ireland) had broken the conditions of peace which had been agreed and had caused havoc in the areas

near the frontiers: the general Lupicinus was sent to deal with the situation with some elements of the mobile strike force. The best documented of the fourth-century disasters in Britain, however, is that of 367, reported fully by the historian Ammianus. Here, the Picts — the Dicalydones and the Verturiones — had linked with other barbarian nations into a full-scale revolt not only on the northern areas but on the southern shores too. Valentinian, then emperor, sent two generals to little avail until Theodosius was chosen. In a carefully measured approach, he reached London, re-established confidence and was able to restore calm: he rebuilt frontier forts and saw to the protection of the province.

It is easy to become carried away both by the account of the severity of this raid in 367 and by the apparent comprehensive steps taken by Theodosius to correct the situation. This Theodosius was the father of the man who had become emperor at the time Ammianus was writing, so there was every reason to maximise his achievements and belittle those of others. There is in all conscience little to show archaeologically for any hostile raids or destruction on the northern frontier in the fourth century: the latest building inscription from Hadrian's Wall which can be dated is the one from Birdoswald of 296–305 recording the rebuilding of the commandant's house, headquarters and baths, but this reflects something of an empire-wide dearth of such inscriptions in the fourth century. Fourth-century buildings have been recognised at various sites, but they are by and large small-scale, and do not reflect a thorough shake-up of the frontier arrangements in the wake of the 'barbarian conspiracy' of 367–8.

One of Theodosius' acts was to disband the *areani*, a class of people who had been appointed in the past but who had become less reliable. Their task had been to travel reasonably long distances, and to tell Roman commanders about any potential trouble among neighbouring tribes. But they had been lured by the prospect of rich rewards through plunder to give the barbarians information about Roman dispositions. The detailed description of these men given by the historian suggests that they were a kind of secret agent who had turned double agent to the detriment of the Romans. At about this time, it appears, all the Roman forts north of Hadrian's Wall were abandoned, and it has often been considered that these *areani* were a network of scouts and informers based in this zone, though other interpretations are possible.

It is difficult to define precisely when the Wall was given up by the Romans. Any one of a number of circumstances might count as the end of Roman control or interest in the area. There may even have been campaigning against the Picts up to the very end of the fourth century. Britain, however, was always of little importance, and troops were withdrawn from the province on several occasions to help bolster rival claims to the imperial throne. By 410, the normally accepted date for the end of Roman Britain, there will have been no further expectation of military help for Britain, nor for official payment of troops stationed there. There is a trickle of coins of the late fourth century from Wall sites, few of them from well-dated contexts, but sufficient to show that there was occupation continuing. Pottery of distinctive late Roman types also appears on several sites, but without something rather better dated (like a sequence of coins) against which to compare its availability, it is not certain how late into the fourth or fifth century this continued to be used. Excavations at one or two sites are beginning to suggest that there was some immediate post-Roman occupation within elements of Wall sites: at Birdoswald, traces of a large post-built hall have been noted on the site of one of the pair of granaries, and built

into its levelled rubble. At South Shields, the complex sequence of ditches outside the west gate and rebuilding of the gate itself in timber suggests that it remained an important defended site until well into the fifth century.

It would be surprising if, on the realisation that no more pay would be forthcoming from the Roman imperial treasury, the Roman inhabitants of the Wall sites, each generation of which had become more farmer than soldier, immediately abandoned their homes and moved away. Roman forts may even have formed the nucleus for settled communities, with the potential for a further build up of local power — a base for the establishment of a kinship group or a clan, and eventually part of the jigsaw that formed itself into the developing Northumbrian Kingdom. Archaeology still has much light to shed on the end of the Roman Wall, but sadly the latest, sometimes most ephemeral, traces of occupation are those which have escaped the attention of past excavators, or are exceptionally difficult to identify. Only by careful and painstaking study has it been possible to piece together something of the complexity of post-Roman occupation at the site of Wroxeter in Shropshire. On the Wall, most of the fort sites have been more disturbed both by past building on them or by past excavations, and the process of piecing together this most illuminating period will be a slow one.

9

Oblivion and rediscovery

The fate of Hadrian's Wall after the Romans has at present to be pieced together from tantalising fragments of information. During the course of the fourth century its function as a barrier had doubtless declined. Manned by troops who were increasingly civilianised, in attitude if not in fact, and whose static nature made active campaigning difficult if not outright impossible, the frontier zone was protected by the establishment of buffer states who could be persuaded by treaty or subsidy to act as early warning of serious trouble. That this system had been in operation for some time is shown by the references to the role of the *areani* (p. 111), and their disbanding for whatever real or imagined offence. All this leaves little physical trace: the difference, in terms of archaeological finds, between a friendly rather than a hostile neighbour might be a greater flow of Roman luxury goods to those who sympathised with Rome's cause. Such arguments can always, however, be stood on their head, for subsidies or payment to keep the peace, which might naturally take this form too, would probably go to unstable as well as stable tribal groups. The finding of Roman luxury goods alone would not be sufficient to show whether the folk who received them were friendly or hostile. In fact, in view of the historians' observations about subsidies and agreements to keep the peace at various times in the third and fourth centuries, there is a surprising dearth of physical signs of any such contact.

Two major tribal groups seem to have occupied the area immediately north of the Wall in the late Roman period. To the west were a tribe called the Selgovae, to the east the Votadini. The exact boundary between their territory is uncertain, but the hill forts of Yeavering Bell and Traprain Law, the latter certainly still occupied at this period, appear definitely to have belonged to the Votadini. Within the ramparts of Traprain Law a large hoard has been found, consisting of late Roman silver treasure, including coin, ingots, and precious artefacts of all sorts, apparently of continental rather than British origin, which could be interpreted as a payment to the tribal chiefs for keeping the peace, or as the proceeds of a successful raiding party, depending on your point of view. Of the two interpretations perhaps the latter is on balance more likely because much of the contents of the hoard had been roughly chopped up or torn apart as if for distribution to a number of recipients.

There is also some evidence, again not archaeological, for more direct Roman intervention in the affairs of these northern tribes. In the post-Roman period, the tribes of lowland Scotland eventually evolved into four tribal dynasties, the earliest Kings in which had Roman names. These names survive within lists, which are ordered compilations of names of men whom tradition (or politically-inspired invention) stretching back into the distant past related to have been Kings. These are notoriously difficult to interpret correctly today. They were often fabricated to prove the connections of existing rulers with famous names of the past, and textually they are sometimes very corrupt. These traditions, whose evidence has accordingly to be taken with more than a pinch of salt, show that these dynasties claimed descent from men with names like Cluim (Clemens), Tacit (Tacitus), Patern (Paternus) or Aetern (Aeternus). Elsewhere on late Roman frontiers, barbarian tribesmen were controlled by Roman officials, set over them as prefects. These names could suggest that the same happened on the northern British frontier, and that such prefects were later regarded by tradition as the founders of a new dynastic succession. This is not, of course, the only interpretation of this evidence which is possible — if one believes in it at all. The Roman sounding names may mean no more than that tribal leaders had begun to embrace Christianity.

Now this is all some way from Hadrian's Wall, but it begins to point to a considerable and continuing Roman finger in the north British pie at the time. If they show anything,

these names suggest that in the earliest days the claim of a Roman name lent the Kings' positions some authority. It would indeed be surprising if the years of Rome's close presence could be so immediately reversed. Nor must it be imagined that the barbarians north of the Wall were an unruly mass, waiting only for the first opportunity of wiping all trace of Rome from their soil: this certainly does not square historically with the picture of Ninian, bishop perhaps of the late Roman diocese of Carlisle, who in the early fifth century took his mission to the northern barbarians and founded a monastery at *Candida Casa* — probably Whithorn — in Galloway. Nor does it chime in well with the slightly later mission of St Patrick to the Irish. To be sure, cross-border raiding was probably a way of life, but there were also civilising influences.

Hadrian's Wall and other structures of Roman Britain could be seen as solid vestiges of an administrative system to which many different elements might cling in the post-Roman period for the security, the authority or the stability

83 *The granaries at Birdoswald fort. Excavated in 1987–8, these granaries were remarkably well preserved beneath the lawn of the farmhouse which stands in the north-west corner of the site. After the northern granary had fallen into disuse, a trench-built rectangular building overlay its site, the clear impression of its foundation trenches cutting through the remains of the stone granary.*

which they gave in times of great change and stress. If this is so, it is clear that the sites could continue to have considerable importance for some time after the 'Roman' period — whenever we consider that to have come to an end. Something of the sort can be seen in the Roman provinces along the River Danube, where historical records relate the exploits of a holy man who, even at the end of the fifth century, was still fostering by military as well as spiritual activity, a Christian Roman lifestyle. Here troops still lived in the forts, always, but apparently vainly, in hope of payment from central funds, and the process of reintegration of 'Roman' with native was well on the road to forming something new and independent of both.

Even where from historical sources we know that something of the sort was happening, archaeology can show little trace of such developments. Recent excavations at Birdoswald have shown that timber buildings occupied the site of the fort granaries after their demolition (83). As yet such developments are undated, but they may be of fifth-century date. They may not, however, in the end be very precisely datable, except that they come later than the final demolition of these major fort buildings. At South Shields, too, work on the ditch system outside the west gate has revealed a complex sequence of defensive improvements — including the cutting of new ditches and possibly the rebuilding of part of the fort gateway in wood — as well as a very late Roman, possibly Christian, cemetery. Tradition has it that South Shields was the birthplace of Oswin, King of Deira, one of the Anglo-Saxon Kingdoms which lay south of the Wall. He was murdered in AD 651, and if the tradition can be believed, it suggests that his family was living at the fort site in the late sixth century.

Archaeological excavations have failed to reveal traces of what was happening there at that date. It is more than possible that nineteenth-century excavations and building on the site have destroyed all traces of this period. At the fort of Newcastle, too, a cemetery occupied the site between the Roman period and the establishment of the castle in AD 1080, though this is not precisely dated, and may be linked with a religious establishment either on the site or nearby. Finally, the find of a fifth- or sixth-century Christian tombstone recording the last resting-place of a man called Brigo-maglos suggests that Vindolanda, too, may still have been occupied (84). Any one of the Roman forts along the Wall could have formed the nucleus of a small tribal group which would appoint its own leaders and might develop a style of existence which could last until well into the fifth or sixth centuries.

The Wall, however, seems to have lost its meaning entirely, and perhaps would have faded completely into history had it not been mentioned in a letter 'On the Ruin of Britain' written by Gildas in the mid-sixth century. Gildas explained the turf wall (the Antonine Wall) as the first response by the Britons to the late Roman incursions by Picts and Scots; unfortunately, he relates, this was insufficient protection, and a second wall, of stone (Hadrian's Wall), was built. This explanation of the two walls, pushing their construction date into the fifth century, perhaps to some extent based on the writer's own experiences of seeing the remains of them, is largely followed by the Venerable Bede in his influential *History of the English Church and People*. This kept the fact of the two walls — but not of course their correct historical context — within the consciousness of those who read their history.

Bede, writing from his monastery in Jarrow, in the late seventh century, clearly had seen the remains of part of Hadrian's Wall: he described it as 8 ft (2.4 m) wide and 12 ft (3.6 m) high, figures which have caused difficulties since later observers related that it was higher than Bede's figure. He wrote at a time when the Northumbrian kingdom was at its strongest, a period when the balance of power lay between east and west — Northumbrian Bernicia in the east, and Cumbrian Rheged in the west. At this period the frontier ran, not east–west along the Wall, but north–south, and its remains are perhaps to be seen in the linear ditch known as the Black Dyke, most noticeable to the north of Sewingshields Crags. Christianity, too, was a major feature of the Northumbrian Kingdom, with the establishment of monasteries at Jarrow, Monkwearmouth, Lindisfarne and churches at Carlisle and Hexham. The Roman Wall and other establishments provided a very convenient source of stone for many of these building projects: the Saxon crypt of the abbey church of St Andrew at Hexham contains a good deal of Roman stone, some of it inscribed, and possibly in origin from Corbridge. But Jarrow and doubtless other buildings of similar

84 *The roughly carved stone, now in Chesters Museum, set up in post-Roman times at Vindolanda to mark the grave of Brigomaglos (the 'M' is upside-down). It has parallels in other early Christian stones from the north which use the same simple formula 'hic iacit', for here lies. In this case the word 'hic' is missing.*

or later date also used convenient Roman stone from the Wall.

The Wall and its forts thus began their slow decline into possible oblivion, stone from the more accessible portions being transported for use elsewhere, while political powers and pressures moved elsewhere in the eighth to tenth centuries, as new waves of invaders from Denmark and Norway threatened established Anglo-Saxon kingdoms. By about the end of the tenth century, the border between England and Scotland began to form in its present position, largely ignoring the line taken by Hadrian's Wall.

The arrival of the Normans in the 1080s brought new pressures to bear on the area: their twin policies of the establishment of royal or local lordships, made explicit by the building of castles, and of the further control of lands through the establishment of monasteries led to more use of available stone from the Wall and its forts. The King's New Castle upon the Tyne was built on the site of the Roman fort of Newcastle in 1080, and, though it was probably around a century before it was converted to stone, this process doubtless led to more collection of Roman material from convenient

nearby sources. Similarly, the establishment of major monastic foundations at Tynemouth, Blanchland, Hexham, Lanercost, Wetheral and Carlisle, will have turned to the nearest convenient sources of building material.

Border unrest was a recurrent feature of the thirteenth to sixteenth centuries, a state of affairs resolved only in the end by the establishment of James I (and VI — of Scotland) on the joint throne of both kingdoms. The years of unrest prior to this led to the establishment of a number of local fortifications both large and small, in the shape both of pele towers and castles, some of which lay in close proximity to the Wall. Prime among these were Thirlwall, Halton, Rudchester, Sewingshields, Corbridge Vicar's Pele, and Drumburgh Castle, all of which again used stone from the Roman remains nearby.

Excavations at Sewingshields milecastle (no 35) have shown something of the pattern of rural settlement in this area (**85**). The Roman milecastle had faded into total disuse before the site was re-used in the thirteenth century, when the first of a series of long narrow 'longhouses' was built on the site (**86**). These provided accommodation for men and animals under the same roof. The remains of three such longhouses, of varying plan when considered in detail, were identified at the site, which appears to have been abandoned in the early decades of the fifteenth century. The site was closely linked with the nearby castle of Sewingshields, successively the property of various local landowners, many of whom held estates elsewhere.

Whether such an exposed spot as the milecastle site was used for anything other than summer pasturage at this period is not known. By the time of a survey of the Wall region conducted in 1542 by Sir Robert Bowes and Sir Ralph Ellerker, however, it was reported that Carrawburgh and Sewingshields were occupied only in summer time for pasture. They went on to recommend that the two 'fortresses' should be re-garrisoned with 'true and honest defensible men' to safeguard the area against the passage of thieves. The land by the sixteenth century was clearly unsafe, occupied only by shielings, shelter for shepherds engaged in summer pasturage, a term which has given the name 'shields' to parts of the upland areas of the Wall. Excavations in the area of Castle Nick milecastle have revealed traces of such hutments clustered together along the back of the wall for shelter against the northern winds, but occupied on a temporary basis only at a period or periods which it is hard to define with any accuracy (see **21**, p. 35).

The union of the crowns of England and Scotland in 1603 did not immediately bring peace to the whole of the border area: for more than a century the whole of the north Tynedale area was still notorious for the activities of men such as the Armstrong family 'notorious thieves and robbers, commonly known as moss-troopers', who lived at Housesteads and whose very presence forced all but the most persistent of the increasing band of antiquarian enquirers

from visiting the site. Several of the remains still visible on the site of Housesteads appear to date from this period: a house stood in the centre of the site, perhaps on the site of the granaries, and a bastle — a strong tower, the later equivalent of the medieval pele-towers —

85 *Medieval fields and earthworks at Sewing-shields. The site of the milecastle and of Sewing-shields Castle at the foot of the crags, the centre of the estate in this area, are both marked. Most of the other earthworks are boundaries, the evidence of other enclosures or traces of agriculture.*

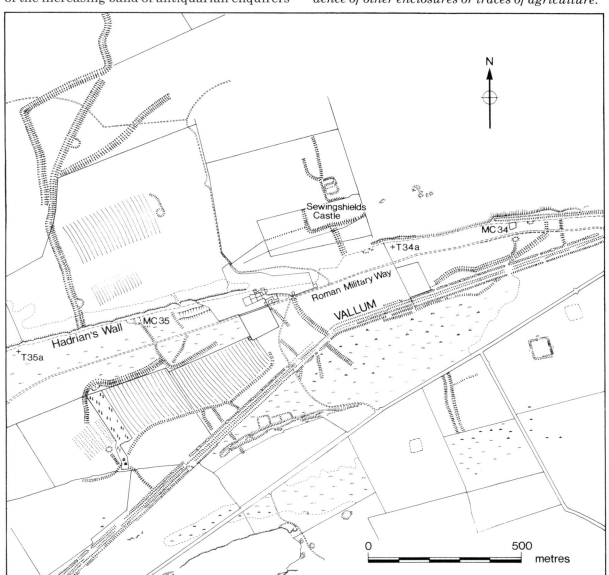

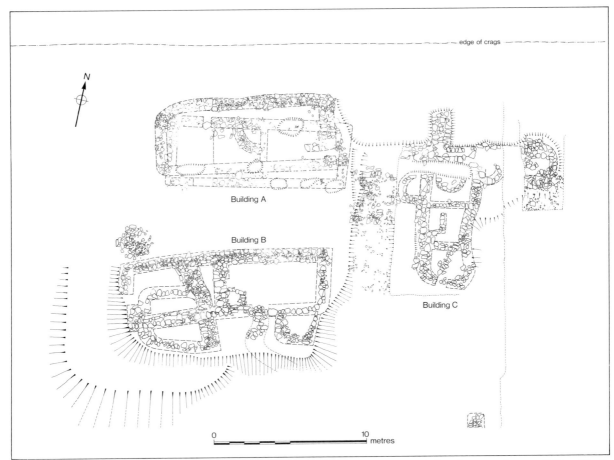

86 *The medieval longhouses at Sewingshields milecastle. The final, thirteenth and fourteenth-century phases at Sewingshields were marked by the implantation within the now totally ruined milecastle of a series of at least three longhouses, one end of which would have been for domestic accommodation, the other for animals.*

was attached to the south gate. Both buildings are associated with large kilns or ovens, both of which can still be seen, one built into the southern granary, the other in the east guard-chamber of the gate. It was only with the sale of Housesteads by the Armstrongs in 1698 to the Gibson family that the era of lawlessness in this area came to an end.

William Camden was the first of the antiquaries to deal extensively with the remains of the Wall, and his *Britannia*, written in Latin, and a history of Britain, not merely the Roman province, went into four editions between 1586 and 1594 before he actually visited the Wall

himself in 1599. His observations of the Wall and some of its sites (he did not go to House-steads for fear of 'the rank robbers thereabouts') generated some interest in the remains, but the main stimulus to further activity, observation, and collection of inscriptional and other evidence from the area had to await the publication of a new edition of *Britannia* in English by Edmund Gibson in 1695 and 1722, which updated Camden's original with considerable 'additions and curious remarks'. Despite the fact that this new edition of the work did not fulfil all it promised, it did act as a considerable spur to further interest in the Wall throughout the eighteenth century. Prime among those was the Rev. John Horsley.

Horsley was a Presbyterian minister, educated in the Grammar School at Newcastle, and graduated from the University of Edinburgh in 1701 where his principal fields of study had been mathematics and philosophy. By 1709 he was a 'dissenting minister' at Morpeth. In between his pursuit of the sciences and the ministerial duties of satisfying the needs of his congregation, Horsley's interests turned to the study of the Roman remains in his neighbourhood.

The noted antiquary William Stukeley, who visited the Wall area in 1725, already looked on Horsley whom he later met as an authority on the Wall. The idea soon formed of compiling a complete corpus of the Roman inscriptions of Britain, prime among which was the wide variety of inscriptions increasingly being discovered along the line of the Wall as interest in the Roman antiquities of the area blossomed, and as an increasing stream of antiquaries passed along the Wall recording what they observed. Horsley's great work, *Britannia Romana*, appeared in three parts: the first volume includes a survey of the remains of the Wall which abounds with the author's own personal observation of the Roman sites in the north — including those of the Antonine Wall in Scotland. Horsley was the first to think historically about the Wall, and the Roman involvement in the whole of northern Britain. He used the available literary evidence of inscriptions and other available sources to assign the forts on the Wall their correct Roman names. The second volume, which involved the greatest labour in the whole exercise, was the collection of around 340 inscriptions and drawings of them which represented a major and primary source for some of this material until the end of the nineteenth century. The third volume incorporated, as something of an afterthought, original documentation on the topography of Roman Britain.

Such a massive undertaking called upon considerable resources from draughtsmen, surveyors and mapmakers to provide the necessary plates to illustrate the work. It was normal for funds for such an enterprise to be raised by public subscription, though there is no trace of any such funding. *Britannia Romana* was at least four years in its progress through the press, finally appearing in April 1732. Unfortunately for the furtherance of eighteenth-century scholarship on the Wall, its author had died three months before it appeared, in January of the same year.

Later travellers and tourists to the Wall area, in the face of such enlightened scholarship on the Roman remains, confined themselves by and large to additional notes on new discoveries.

During the course of the eighteenth century, however, despite the awakening of interest in the Wall and its antiquities — partly no doubt inspired by contemporary discoveries at Herculaneum and Pompeii in Italy which were receiving considerable attention — the pace of destruction to the Wall and its remains was quickened. In 1745, Charles Stuart marched into England down the western route, passing through Brampton. The ease with which the Jacobites entered England had its consequence in the construction of a new lateral road by General Wade which was to link Newcastle and Carlisle. Despite urgent pleas from antiquaries like Stukeley, this road, whose course is largely followed by the present-day B6318, utilised the levelled foundations and lower courses of the Roman Wall for most of the first 30 or so miles (48 km) out of Newcastle as its base (**87**). The road only leaves the line of the Wall finally where it begins to rise up to the crags of Sewingshields. In occupying the site of the Wall, however, it has preserved its course in a way which might otherwise have been impossible. East of Carlisle, where the Wall's course runs through similar pastureland, its course has been thoroughly obliterated by the gradual and insistent demands of agriculture.

87 *Hadrian's Wall exposed in the road surface at Walwick Bank, near Chesters; the construction of General Wade's military road in the years following 1745 made use of the broad foundation of the Wall for about the first 30 miles (50 km) or so out of Newcastle. In places, as this engraving shows, the foundations of the Wall were still visible within the road surface, and doubtless still survive beneath the modern tarmac.*

Pressures of this sort, however, gradually revealed the need for a record to be made of sections of the Wall or its constituent forts as they were uncovered. At Benwell in 1751/2, as the new road was passing by, plans of the fort and of its external bathhouse, uncovered in the construction work, were drawn by Robert Shafto. For much of the eighteenth century, however, such exploration as there was on the Roman Wall was confined to accidental discoveries or occasional curiosities which were retained for view to the passing visitor: excavations at Housesteads in 1724 caused it to be described as the 'Tadmor of Britain', a reference to the site's prolific number of inscribed stones and statues, and the then current publication of visits by other learned antiquaries to sites fringing the Mediterranean Sea, including that of Tadmor (Palmyra) itself.

The beginnings of more methodical excavation had to wait until the nineteenth century. This was begun by Rev. John Hodgson in the early decades of the century, but the study of Wall sites was fostered in earnest by the burgeoning interest of members of the Society of Antiquaries of Newcastle upon Tyne, newly formed in 1813. Pleas for more scientific examination of the Roman sites along the Wall were followed by the start of excavations at Housesteads and at Vindolanda. The greatest impetus to the study of the Wall by excavation was, however, given by John Clayton, the owner of the Chesters estate. Between 1832 and his death in 1890, a considerable portion of his spare time was devoted to the excavation and protection of the remains of the Roman Wall — at the time of his death he was the owner of five of the major Roman sites in the area and was concerned to secure their preservation. His energies also went into the enhancement of the collection of antiquities from many different sites which is still housed at Chesters.

John Clayton's excavations were directed at the exploration of many of the better-known sites on the Wall. These included the investigation of parts of the forts or their surrounding buildings at Housesteads (1849 and following), Carrawburgh (1873–6), and Carvoran (1886). In addition, he instigated excavation work at the milecastles of Cawfields in 1848 and at Housesteads milecastle in 1853, as well as at Turret 29a (Black Carts). One of the most spectacular finds was that of the well of Coventina at Carrawburgh, where excavation began in 1876.

In addition, virtually all that can be seen of the fort of Chesters today, including the remains of the Roman bridge across the Tyne, was the product of work he instigated.

Clayton himself was responsible for the establishment of Chesters as an archaeological site with remains which could be inspected by visitors, and within the estate there was a small garden pavilion in which some of the more notable finds — from Chesters and elsewhere — were displayed. At his death in 1890, some attempts were made to catalogue these and to establish with as much accuracy as was then possible where they had originally come from. Eventually, Nathaniel Clayton commissioned a permanent museum to house the antiquities. This museum, completed in 1896, together with the collection it contains, has remained virtually unaltered to the present day, and still therefore retains the spirit and period flavour in the presentation of his collection of which John Clayton would doubtless have approved.

Meanwhile threats were not slow to materialise, particularly at the eastern end of the Wall where the latter part of the nineteenth century brought prosperity to Newcastle. In 1858, the northern third of the fort at Benwell was ripped away for the construction of a new reservoir. In 1874, the Church Commissioners put forward plans to develop the site of South Shields fort for housing, but as a result of public subscription excavations took place on the site beforehand, with the result that the central part of the site was left clear of houses and a small museum collection established. Wallsend, also covered by housing in the 1880s, was unluckier: only later keyhole excavation supplemented the small amount of prior excavation which had been permitted. In the nature of things, however, all such developments can prove to be transitory, for in the 1980s both Wallsend and South Shields forts have resurfaced from beneath the Victorian terraced housing to see renewed excavation, research and display.

The nineteenth-century style of excavation, which consisted largely in the examination of stone structures, and the chasing of walls and outlines of buildings without great recourse to what would today be regarded as the necessary archaeological methods or the detailed recording of sequences and stratigraphy, the careful provenancing of all finds, and the collection of all forms of samples of excavated material, lasted at many Wall sites up until the outbreak

of the First World War. This interrupted an early series of excavations at Corbridge (1906–14) which had appalled the young Leonard Wooley who had worked there in their first season. Excavations by Bosanquet in 1898 at Housesteads, however (88), had in a very brief space of time produced something unknown before in Roman studies — the complete plan of a Roman fort: even though a great deal of this must be conjectural, the plan is a classic which was still used almost up to the present to guide visitors round the fort. Only much more recent detailed work has begun to supplement and alter some of its main outlines.

The pioneer of newer and more revealing excavation techniques in the Wall area was F G Simpson, whose examination of Haltwhistle Burn fortlet, its associated watermill, and several of the Wall structures, including milecastle 48 (Poltross Burn) was undertaken before war broke out. Research on many aspects of the Wall was by 1920 beginning in earnest, with the development of a programme of excavation to test various research questions about the Wall and the vallum. A North of England Excavation Committee was formed in 1924: this

88 *Housesteads excavations, 1899. A small number of original photographs of Bosanquet's excavation at Housesteads survive, and this one shows well the style of 'wall-chasing' which was used. It produced a virtually complete plan of the buildings within the fort, but failed to show the complexities of all the alterations which had taken place.*

concentrated primarily on excavation work in the east of the Wall, examining the sites of turrets and milecastles, as well as responding to yet another major threat of housing, this time over the southern portion of the fort of Benwell. To the west, the Cumberland Excavation Committee was also in full swing, with Simpson as their main excavations director. To these bodies were added the Durham University Excavation Committee. The work done by these three bodies in the 1920s and 1930s, and, still more important, the prompt publication within the pages of the relevant local journals, did more than anything else to set most of the Hadrian's Wall sites which visitors can see today firmly on the archaeological map, as well as forming new conclusions about the nature of Hadrian's frontier, some of which have stood the test of time, but all of which have provided fresh stimulus to more recent research.

In 1849, John Collingwood Bruce had led the first pilgrimage along Hadrian's Wall: the enterprise was taken up, if not on a regular basis, by the two northern societies, in Newcastle and in Cumberland. A centenary pilgrimage took place in 1949: this was able to present to a large and interested audience the results from the excavations immediately prior to the Second World War. By now, a number of the most important sites had been offered and accepted into the care of the Ministry of Works: most notable, perhaps, was the central portion of the site at Corbridge, where clearance work of the remains was undertaken ready for their display to the public. In the post-war years, this led to a renewal of interest in the site as a whole, and to a more comprehensive series of excavations which only came to an end in 1976, and which was aimed at the examination of earlier fort structures beneath the stone layout.

Modern excavation techniques, however, by their greater thoroughness and cost made it less and less feasible to keep up the pace of research established in the 1920s and 1930s. Opportunities were taken to examine new sites as chance made them available — as in the case of the Temple of Mithras at Carrawburgh in 1949–50. The constraints of funding, however, have meant that in more recent years excavation or detailed survey have only been possible on those sites which are either laid out for visitors to view — such as Housesteads, Corbridge or South Shields — or where there is a threat to the existing remains which makes them candidates for recording prior to new development: thus the fort of Wallsend, cleared of its nineteenth-century terraced housing, was excavated prior to the intended implantation of light industry on the site. More enlightened decisions have now ensured that the fort site is spared this further indignity, but the excavation took place just the same.

Modern excavation work is labour-intensive: whereas the 'keyhole' archaeological techniques of the past threw up relatively rapid answers to questions posed of the evidence — essential clues in the piecing together of a masterpiece of detection — such solutions are no longer regarded as entirely satisfactory. Not only are many sites excavated in the past now known to be far more complex than was realised even in the 1930s, but a balanced assessment of the quantity of artefacts and evidence they produce normally requires more study. Publication therefore can rarely follow as immediately on discovery as it did in earlier days and the need to comprehend adequately the results from one site necessarily gives pause before commencing work at another.

Excavation on the Wall is, therefore, a continuing process of measured discovery: it continually feeds off the collected results of the past. But it is not undertaken for the sheer joy of finding new 'treasures'. The point of the exercise — and this applies whether it is a response to a development threat, or whether it affords the prospect of fresh remains which help interpret a site for visitors — is to enhance our overall knowledge about the past. It is an experiment which has to be carefully planned to ensure that the information gleaned is of greatest use: the excavator who sticks his spade in the ground ought to know what evidence he is looking for and why he seeks it. Even on Hadrian's Wall, after the great weight of scholarship and research expended on the subject since the days of John Horsley, new discoveries are still being made which, in the most healthy way possible, ensure that past doctrines and theories about the Wall are continually kept under review.

10
The Wall today and in the future

The complex of structures, forts, and earthwork remains of the Roman period make Hadrian's Wall and its landscape one of the most important combinations of archaeological remains of any period in the world. International recognition of this was gained in 1987, when the remains of Hadrian's frontier in Britain were inscribed on the World List of cultural monuments compiled by UNESCO.

Yet its very complexity and completeness present a number of problems which have to be faced today. Archaeological remains are vulnerable: they can be disturbed by development — the construction of new roads, the laying of telephone cables, the building or extending of a barn — or by agricultural pro-

cesses like ploughing, drainage or tree-planting. There have therefore to be safeguards which aim at the protection of archaeological remains, whether standing or buried, from this sort of damage. Archaeological sites contain information about their construction and use, about their processes of decay and abandonment, which can be extracted under the correct con-

89 *West of Housesteads fort, the Wall runs through some of the most spectacular scenery on its line. Some of these portions still remain as they were rebuilt in the nineteenth or early twentieth century, with the facing stones replaced round the Roman core to form a flat top, just over a metre high.*

90 *The Irthing gorge, just south of Birdoswald fort, provides a beautiful landscape feature within the estate which also includes the fort. This is all now in the ownership of Cumbria County Council, who are developing plans to enable visitors to appreciate the natural as well as the archaeological resource at this spot.*

ditions, and which can thus form the framework for a better understanding of the Roman past.

But the Wall country is not all archaeology. Concern for the landscape value of the Wall and its setting (**89, 90**), for its associative value for visitors, or for the aesthetic appeal of the remains as one now finds them must also form part of today's attempts to protect and preserve. The Wall's importance as a national cultural resource brings its own pressures for tourism and various forms of exploitation. The prospect of economic development and the provision of necessary services for visitors have to be handled sensitively and carefully so as not to change the very character of the landscape people wish to study and enjoy.

Thus the Wall today needs to be protected on two main fronts. First, from processes which

may affect its most precious and vulnerable resource, the archaeological remains, and second, from changes which may lead to an alteration to the essential character of the Wall landscape. Coordination of an approach which seeks to steer between all the available pitfalls in these areas rests with local and national authorities. As far as the archaeology of the Wall is concerned, protection means leaving remains undisturbed if at all possible: in that way, the information they contain is safe. For the Wall landscape positive steps to conserve its character are continually necessary: this is the essence of countryside management, and discordant elements which fail to match the existing surroundings are discouraged.

English Heritage has an important part to play in these processes of protection. Most of the line of Hadrian's Wall and its associated Roman remains is one of the monuments protected by law. All applications received for any operations which might affect the Wall are carefully monitored, and consent is only recommended if sites are not in danger of damage, or if adequate steps have been taken, for example by excavation, to ensure that information which

may be uncovered as part of the operation is properly recorded.

It is not always practicable, however, to insist that the Wall and its remains are kept free of all disturbance. Portions of the Wall run through heavily built-up areas of Newcastle and Carlisle, and, particularly at the west end of the Wall, there are small villages, like Bowness or Burgh by Sands, actually on the site of the Wall or its forts. Some development in these areas, either in the form of new buildings for office or residential use, or in the provision of new services for existing buildings, has often to be faced. Whilst every effort is made to minimise the impact of these modern pressures to the Wall, it is not always possible to divert them or to negotiate alternative solutions which will protect the archaeological remains from disruption.

Hadrian's Wall crosses England from sea to sea. Some services, among them gas pipelines, telephone cables, or other service trenches will always have to run north to south across the line of the Wall to supply modern needs (**92**). It is not always possible to insist on their diversion past the Wall through corridors where the archaeological remains have already been badly disturbed, and where little or no further damage will be done. Sometimes such schemes have avoided the problem by thrust-boring

91 *Greatchesters fort from the air; Hadrian's Wall enters the photograph at bottom right, and runs across to a point mid left; for much of this distance its ditch is clearly to be seen. Greatchesters fort lies just south of the farm buildings, which encroach on its north-east corner. Large modern barns have been built just outside the northern side of the fort, in part overlying its ditch.*

under the Wall, leaving the archaeology intact above, although this is not always an acceptable or practicable solution.

Other modern pressures arise from the familiar problems of the economic use by the farming community of land which contains significant archaeological remains. The land-use along most of the Wall's line is pasture, normally regarded as the best way of safeguarding the buried remains. Despite this, there may be demands for farming operations such as drainage, or for the construction of barns and other agricultural buildings to take place in areas known to contain Roman remains or earthworks (**91**). To take just one example, if a pasture field is to stay in good condition, it must normally be grazed by animals, and the supply of water for drinking troughs through pipes laid in the ground has therefore to be considered. If the pasture field happens to contain the remains

125

92 *Rescue archaeology on the Wall: turret 10a at Throckley, near Newcastle. Proposals to install a new sewerage system beneath the road which follows the line of Hadrian's Wall led to the rediscovery of this turret in 1980, as well as revealing the extent to which it had been disturbed since its discovery in 1928. It is crossed by a water main and by a water-pipe connected to a fire hydrant. Its discovery and full excavation, however, led to a decision to direct the sewerage scheme round it rather than through it, as originally planned.*

of a Roman fort, ways have to be found of accommodating the need to protect the remains by keeping them safely under pasture, and the provision of water for stock which may be helping to keep the pasture well-managed. Careful decisions continually have to be taken about whether the archaeological resource or the modern needs of farming are the more important.

Other problems arise from the presence of large numbers of visitors in particular in the central sectors of the Wall. There are areas here where the Wall, although it is buried, can be at risk from erosion as people scramble up or down the steep slopes up which it sometimes climbs. A recent programme of excavation in

the area of the Castle Nick milecastle was aimed at preventing this kind of unconscious damage. The solution adopted was to excavate the Wall and expose and consolidate it, thus ensuring that visitors could see it (**93–4**). Combined with the provision of a footpath nearby, it was hoped that the erosion would thus be prevented.

In one sense, it is only through excavation that more will be learnt about the Wall, but it is also true that all archaeological excavation causes damage to the remains. Where the remains of the Wall are at risk from destruction or damage, excavation, as a controlled way of carrying out and recording the damaging

93 *Castle Nick milecastle prior to excavation work. In 1983 a programme of excavation and survey began on the section of Wall owned by the National Trust near Castle Nick milecastle (no 39), aimed at arresting the damage and erosion caused to the buried remains of the Wall by walkers scrambling up the steep slopes of the dip within which the milecastle lay.*

94 *After excavation of the Wall and of portions of the milecastle, the Wall was consolidated and a new footpath laid next to it so that walkers can climb the steep slopes more easily and avoid the remains.*

process is better than nothing but it does not preserve except as a record on paper. The main thrust of the protection of the Wall is to avoid unnecessary destruction of the archaeological resource. This is sometimes seen as a rather curious point of view by those who see archaeology as a means of continual discovery. Leaving things safely buried and undisturbed to them may seem to be a denial of the essential questioning which keeps interest in the past alive: but there are good reasons for it.

First, the pace of change, and the pressure for beneficial use of all land is perhaps greater now than at any time in the past. This poses threats to archaeological sites of all kinds, not merely Hadrian's Wall, and the annual budget available to fund the examination of sites prior to their destruction by excavation is a limited one. Encouraging moves have been made in recent years as owners and developers begin to recognise that the cost of recording the sites they perforce destroy through development schemes should be carried within their overall project costs: but even so the extent to which English Heritage grants, ultimately derived from the taxpayer, have to support this necessary archaeological work does not noticeably diminish. Even now, not all such threats can be answered by an excavation. Every case where the need for excavation can be avoided both safeguards the evidence intact for the future and saves money — for other more urgent requirements.

Second, as it has already been pointed out, excavation is a damaging process. It is perhaps not as easy to grasp this point when, on Hadrian's Wall, there is still so much of the Roman structure of the Wall to examine at first hand. To understand a building in its context, it is necessary to examine what lies under it, round it, and on top of it: this means looking in detail at the collapse of its roof or upper portions, analysing its structural detail, floor levels, evidence for internal partitions and the like, as well as studying its foundations in relationship to anything which preceded it. From such an exercise, material such as coins, pottery or metalwork, which might be able to give a valuable indication of date, and other finds such as bone or soil samples, which can illuminate questions of climatic or local environmental conditions, can be recovered. This exercise can only be carried out once — the way in which layers and levels have been laid down is part of the history of the site which can be interpreted only during excavation, and never recreated.

The destruction of this information resource is a serious matter: if it is done in an uncontrolled way, the information on what has happened in the past is lost altogether. The only controlled way of doing this is, however, by the time-consuming process of excavation. While this seeks to maximise the amount of information recovered, it is only as good as current practice and study can make it. Techniques for the recovery of information have improved beyond measure in the last 100 years, and significantly in the last thirty. The recognition of new techniques of understanding the evidence is taking place all the time. There is much to be said, therefore, for desisting from excavation where it is not absolutely necessary in order that, perhaps in 100 years' time, greater benefit and understanding will be derived from the study of a particular site.

Altruistic this may sound, but it is important to recognise that we are all custodians of the remains of the past. We cannot hope to understand everything about the Roman frontier, but research questions will continue to be asked, and selective excavations will take place in order to achieve a measured response to current problems and difficulties. These should be concentrated on only a small fraction of the archaeological resource, and much of our energies therefore will also go into the rather more negative aspects of ensuring that there are areas of the Roman resource on Hadrian's Wall left untouched by our activities for future exploration and enjoyment. This is archaeologist's dilemma and the area where the need for a responsible approach to conservation and preservation is paramount.

There is, however, a far more immediate and practical side to English Heritage's work on Hadrian's Wall. Its responsibilities there are more wide-ranging than merely those of seeking to minimise the impact of any work which may be damaging to the archaeological heritage. Besides this, it is directly responsible for the management of a number of properties on the Wall, an 'estate' which includes approximately 4 miles ($6\frac{1}{2}$ km) of curtain wall, 7 milecastles, and 14 turrets, as well as a number of other structures, for example the Temple of Mithras at Carrawburgh, or the Vallum Causeway at Benwell. In addition it also looks after three of the major sites in the Wall zone, the Wall forts

95 *Hadrian's Wall at Walltown Crags in November 1958, before masons moved in to begin clearance and consolidation.*

of Housesteads and Chesters, and a portion of the Roman town of Corbridge.

At all of these, it has a duty not only to care for and consolidate the remains, but also properly to understand them and thus to be able to present them fully and intelligently to visitors of all ages. This is particularly difficult to achieve successfully at a site like Corbridge, where several different periods of buildings are still visible and can easily cause confusion. It also poses problems at other sites, for example at Housesteads, in deciding how best to lay out the results of recent excavation work to allow them to be understood. Here the remains of fourth century barrack-blocks overlie the traces of the original Hadrianic layout, and any attempt to display a multiplicity of different phases of Roman use of the same site could cause considerable confusion to the visitor. The earlier layouts have therefore been suppressed in favour of the late Roman arrangements.

The way in which the remains of the Wall and its structures are consolidated as ruins has been established as one in which they are treated 'as found' (**95–6**). This first involves the careful clearance of the Roman structures from the soil or vegetation surrounding them, a process which today is always accompanied by archaeological recording and exploration, though this was not always considered necessary in the past. The ruined walls then have to be capped to prevent water getting in from the top: the wall-top is finished in rough rubble stone set in mortar, similar to the original Roman wall-core, and the pointing of the surviving facing stones of the Roman walls with a weak mixture of lime, sand and cement. Every care is taken to ensure that stones consolidated in this way for display are left in the same relationship to each other as they were when first found. This enables significant relationships and evidence to be re-examined at first hand.

The whole process, however, of displaying the remains of the Wall and its structures is a necessary compromise. What it seeks to do is to arrest the gradual processes of decay at a

129

96 *The same stretch of Wall in 1960, after treatment.*

particular moment — normally the moment when the remains were first dug up — without adding any form of modern interpretation to the structure which may confuse or mislead visitors or invite the derision or criticism of future generations. Often the reasons for doing this are as much concerned with the preservation of the Roman fabric as they are with the display of the Wall: during the course of the nineteenth century, John Clayton carried out excavations on parts of the curtain wall of Hadrian's Wall. In many places he discovered that the mortared core of the Wall survived rather better than the worked faces, which had often fallen off, and

lay in a tumble of stones at the Wall's foot. His solution to the problems of how to preserve the original Roman fabric was to rebuild the wall-faces around the core with those readily available facing stones, and to cap the whole new structure with a flat surface — sometimes of soil or cinders which could form a footpath.

Though fine for its day, this solution begins now to raise other problems: the volume of visitors to the Wall makes the pressure of walkers on the Wall's top far greater than it was in Clayton's day. In places, the reconstructed walls are beginning to bulge, and, in many cases, the rebuild was so carefully matched to the original that it is difficult to tell what is Roman work *in situ* and what is Clayton's rebuilt Wall. To the visitor this may not matter, but to the archaeologist whose concern is with the primacy of original evidence in its undisturbed position this matters a great deal, as does the need to preserve the undisturbed core-portions of the Wall where these survive behind Clayton's rebuilding. Since walking on the Wall contributes to the problems of maintenance, English Heritage, along with other responsible bodies like the National Trust, is attempting to divert visitors from the Wall top on to footpaths placed beside the Wall wherever possible.

This is just one example of the problems caused by the attempt to stop the processes of decay at a given artificial moment in the history of a site, and it has to be admitted that a great deal of ingenuity goes into the process of ensuring that the truncated remains are weatherproof and as accurate as possible. All such consolidation, however, involves a certain amount of interference with the remains, if only by the insertion of modern pointing into areas where Roman mortar has perished. Such work is continually necessary to enable the educational potential of the sites on the Wall to be fulfilled, although there is a fine line to tread between the falsification of evidence and the honesty of techniques of display and layout which show the visitor what was found exactly as it was discovered.

97 *The reconstructed west gateway at South Shields fort. First excavated in part in the nineteenth century, the remains of this gate were fully examined by modern excavation before this replica was placed on the site. It has been fully researched from surviving examples of Roman gates elsewhere (including those on Hadrian's Wall, see 32–3). It is certainly a very impressive reminder of the size and scale of the Roman buildings which rose from the foundations still to be seen in many places.*

It is in this light that one must view with a certain amount of unease the current fashion, still marginally more prevalent on the Continent than in Britain, for the reconstruction of Roman or other monuments to a modern-day conception of their original full size and shape. Reconstructions such as the west gate of the fort at South Shields are certainly impressive, and they show better than any model the full-scale of the Roman structures whose foundations are so similar (**97**). Educationally, therefore, it can be agreed, they fulfil a very valuable function, as well as attracting more and more people to a site which otherwise might be considered little worth their time and attention. These are valid arguments, but the unease about the whole process springs from a number of other considerations: first, the primacy of real evidence about the Roman period on Hadrian's Wall and the north. A reconstruction is a fiction, however well researched, and from an archaeological viewpoint it is better for people to look at real rather than made-up evidence. Second, the process of construction of such structures — if placed on original sites — necessitates a degree of violence to the remains which is just as damaging as if the structure placed upon them is a car-park, a new school or a public convenience. Third, such developments have a snowball effect: once one is in place, there is a tendency for other, rival, structures to compete for visitors' attention on other sites. It would be a pity, in an area which is so full of the genuine Roman article for a rash of 'simulated' Roman remains to rise like mushrooms on every Roman site. Quite apart from the horrendous costs involved — themselves an important indication of the Romans' own input into construction schemes — such reconstructed remains often date quickly, as new research points new interpretations to old problems. That is a path down which, on balance, it seems better not to go.

The continuing need to care for the archaeological resource of Hadrian's Wall is one which demands a high degree of commitment to, and respect for, the Roman past. It cannot be carried out without close cooperation with farmers, owners, visitors, and public bodies, both locally and nationally. Its primary aim is to safeguard the remains for the future, whilst seizing, in as appropriate and as sensitive a manner as possible, on proposals which will result in maximising people's enjoyment from their visits to the Wall. If, in doing so, it is possible to use the Wall, its structures, and its landscape to increase people's awareness of their heritage, to inform them as to its true character and significance, and to encourage them to give support in the task of looking after it for the future, a major task will have been achieved.

Further reading

There is a large volume of books and other literature on Hadrian's Wall. Of these, two are undoubtedly the most important: *Hadrian's Wall* by David Breeze and Brian Dobson, first published in 1976, but now in its third (Pelican paperback) edition; and the *Handbook to the Roman Wall* originally published by J Collingwood Bruce, but last revised, in its thirteenth edition, in 1978 by Charles Daniels. The former is a full review of the available evidence for the Wall which takes a broadly historical approach. The latter, since its beginning in 1863, has always been a guidebook for visitors, and the latest edition provides succint descriptions of not only the Wall-sites themselves, but also a large number of other associated Roman sites in the north. Each of them has a large and reasonably comprehensive bibliography organised according to themes and sites respectively: to these the reader of the present volume should turn for detailed information on particular sites.

The historical sources about the Wall and the northern frontier are most conveniently gathered together in J C Mann (ed) *The Northern frontier in Britain from Hadrian to Honorius: literary and epigraphic sources*, and the wider perspective, setting Hadrian's Wall in its British context, is best given by general works on Roman Britain such as Sheppard Frere's *Britannia*, now (1987) in its third edition, by Peter Salway's *Roman Britain*, part of the Oxford History of England, (1981), or by Malcolm Todd's *Roman Britain, 55 BC–AD 400* (1981).

In the abbreviated bibliography which follows, I have tried to give a selection of books or articles which provide fruitful avenues for the development of themes touched on in the separate chapters of this book. Much of the detailed work on the Wall has been published in the annual proceedings of the two local archaeological and historical societies most closely involved with the north of England. The *Transactions of the Cumberland and Westmorland Antiquarian and Archaeological Society* and *Archaeologia Aeliana* (*AA* in the references below), the annual publication of the Society of Antiquaries of Newcastle upon Tyne, carry between them a large number of important studies on Wall-sites certainly in this century, and in some cases in the nineteenth century too. Many important papers on subjects connected with Wall-themes are also to be found in the annual journal *Britannia* (not to be confused with Sheppard Frere's book) published by the Society for the Promotion of Roman Studies.

1 The Wall and its setting
General works on Roman frontiers are few and far between, and much published material on other Roman frontiers is in languages other than English. The best recent survey comes in the compilation of essays edited by J Wacher entitled *The Roman World* (1987), with sections by different authors on frontiers in mainland Europe, Britain, Africa and the East (pp 139–325), and includes a comprehensive bibliography. A general view of Roman frontiers is given in G Webster *The Roman Imperial Army,* (3rd ed 1985). For a view of the tactics of the Roman frontiers, see Edward N Luttwak, *The Grand Strategy of the Roman Empire (1976)*.

2 The build-up to the Wall
The Brigantes: W S Hanson and D B Campbell, The Brigantes: from clientage to conquest, *Britannia* xvii (1986), 73–90.

On Stanwick: R E M Wheeler, *The Stanwick Fortifications* (1945).

Agricola: R M Ogilvie and I A Richmond (eds) *Cornelii Taciti de vita Agricolae* (1967) — text, commentary and translation of Tactitus's life of Agricola. See also W S Hanson *Agricola* (1987), and *Scottish Archaeological Forum 12*, for a series of papers on Agricola's career.

On forts in Scotland: D J Breeze, *Roman Scotland* (1979), and the early chapters of W Hanson and G Maxwell *Rome's North West frontier: the Antonine Wall* (1983).

Corbridge: W Hanson and others, 'The Agricolan supply base at Red House, Corbridge', *AA* series 5, vii (1979), 1–88; on the fort site beneath the present remains, M W Bishop and J N Dore *Excavations at Roman Corbridge; the site* (1988).

The Stanegate forts: E Birley, *Research on Hadrian's Wall* (1961), 132 f; G D B Jones, *Britannia* xiii (1982), 283f.

On finds at Vindolanda: R Birley *Vindolanda* (1977) esp pp 103–57; on the writing tablets, A K Bowman and J D Thomas *Vindolanda: the Latin writing-tablets* (1983): and, by the same authors, 'New texts from Vindolanda', *Britannia* xviii (1987), 125–42.

The Corbridge hoard: M W Bishop and L Allason-Jones, *Excavations at Roman Corbridge: the hoard* (1988).

3 The Wall is begun

Much the best reference works on the individual Wall structures and the building of the wall are to be found in the general works listed at the beginning of the bibliography. Chapter 2 of Breeze and Dobson's *Hadrian's Wall* in particular gives a succinct account of the building, but also spells out the problems of modern interpretation; chapter II of C M Daniels's edition of the *Handbook* gives a rapid view of the evidence.

Also of importance are more detailed studies: C E Stevens *The Building of Hadrian's Wall* (1966); J Hooley and D J Breeze, 'The building of Hadrian's Wall: a reconsideration' *AA* series 4, 46 (1968), 97f.

For recent work on the Wall's bridges: P T Bidwell and N Holbrook *The bridges of Hadrian's Wall* (1989).

4 The forts are added

On Roman forts in general: A Johnson *Roman Forts* (1983); G Webster *The Roman Imperial Army* (1985).

The forts on Hadrian's Wall: D J Breeze and B Dobson 'Fort types on Hadrian's Wall, *AA* series 4, 47 (1969), 15f.

The vallum: B Heywood, 'The vallum — its problems restated', in *Britain and Rome* (ed M G Jarrett and B Dobson) 1966, 85f.

5 What was the Wall for?

Most general works on Roman Britain have to face this problem; S S Frere, *Britannia* 111–122, P Salway *Roman Britain* 175–185, and M Todd *Roman Britain 55 BC–AD 400*, 138–49 all discuss the problems, and they are further treated in the general works mentioned at the head of this 'further reading' section. More recently, B Dobson 'The function of Hadrian's Wall', in *AA* series 5, 14 (1986), 5–30, has given a thorough review of the question.

On the Brigantes and their background: C Haselgrove 'The later pre-Roman Iron Age between the Humber and the Tyne', in *Settlement and Society in the Roman North* (eds P R Wilson, R F J Jones and D M Evans), 1984, 9–25.

6 Abandonment and reoccupation

On the move northwards to the Antonine Wall: W S Hanson and G Maxwell *Rome's North-West frontier, the Antonine Wall* (1985).

The construction of the Antonine Wall: G S Maxwell 'Fortlets and distance-slabs on the Antonine Wall' *Britannia* xvi (1985), 25–8.

Modifications to Hadrian's Wall; V A Maxfield and R Miket, 'The excavation of turret 33b (Coesike)', *AA* series 4, 50 (1972) 158f.

Sewingshields milecastle: D Haigh and M Savage 'Excavations at milecastle 35 (Sewingshields)' *AA* series 5, 12 (1984), 33–147.

The history of the frontier in this period: J P Gillam and J C Mann, 'The northern British frontier from Antonius Pius to Caracalla' *AA* series 4, 48 (1970), 1–44; J P Gillam 'The frontier after Hadrian — a history of the problem', *AA* series 5, 2 (1974), 1–15.

7 Civilians on the Wall

On conditions of life for the Roman soldier in general: G R Watson, *The Roman Soldier* (1969); R W Davies (ed D J Breeze and V A Maxfield) *Service in the Roman Army* (1987).

The Iron Age background: see the papers in *Settlement and society in the Roman North* (eds P R Wilson, R F J Jones and D M Evans), 1984; N Higham, *The northern counties to AD 1000*, 1987; G Jobey, 'Homesteads and settlements of the frontier area', in *Rural settlement in Roman Britain* (ed C Thomas), 1966, 1–14, together with a succession of later papers by the same author on the pre-Roman periods in the Tyne–Forth area conveniently listed in Higham's book 360–2.

On the supply of the Roman army: D J Breeze, 'Demand and supply on the northern frontier', in *Between and beyond the Walls* (ed C Burgess and R Miket), 1984, pp 264–86.

Roman settlements round forts: P Salway, *The frontier people of Roman Britain* (1965); R Birley, *Civilians on the Roman frontier* (1983); R Birley, *Vindolanda, a Roman frontier post on Hadrian's Wall* (1977); Sebastian Sommer *The military vici of Roman Britain*, British Archaeological Reports 129 (1984).

Coventina's Well, Carrawburgh: L Allason-Jones and B McKay, *Coventina's Well* (1985).

Mithraism: C M Daniels *Mithras and his temples on the Wall* (1967).

The Carrawburgh mithraeum: J P Gillam and I A Richmond 'The mithraeum at Carrawburgh', *AA* series 4, 29 (1950), 1ff.

8 The static frontier

For general works on the third and fourth centuries on the frontier, see Breeze and Dobson's *Hadrian's Wall*, and the works by J P Gillam and J C Mann cited under chapter 6 of this further reading section above.

Vindolanda: P T Bidwell, *The Roman fort of Vindolanda* (1986).

South Shields: J N Dore and J P Gillam, *The Roman fort at South Shields* (1979); recent excavations by P T Bidwell have been reported on in annual summaries in *Britannia*, xvi (1985), 268; xvii (1986), 347–7; xviii (1987), 315.

Milecastles: for Milecastle 35 (Sewingshields), see the paper by D Haigh and M Savage listed under chapter 6 above; work at Milecastle 39 by J G Crow has been reported in *Britannia* xvii (1986), 378–381 and viii (1987), 316, and in *Current Archaeology* 108 (Feb 1988), 14–17.

Hadrian's Wall bridges: P T Bidwell and N Holbrook *The Bridges of Hadrian's Wall* (1989).

Barrack accommodation at Wallsend and elsewhere: C M Daniels, 'Excavations at Wallsend and the fourth century barracks on Hadrian's Wall', in W Hanson and L Keppie, *Roman Frontier Studies 12*, British Archaeological Reports S 71 (1980) 173f.

The end of the Wall: J C Mann 'The northern frontier after AD 369', *Glasgow Archaeological Journal*, 3 (1974) 34–42.

9 Oblivion and rediscovery

In general on the progress of past work on the Wall: E Birley, *Research on Hadrian's Wall* (1961), which gives a very full picture of the state of research up to that point.

The text of Gildas can most conveniently be found in *Gildas: Arthurian Period Sources vol 7* edited and translated by M Winterbottom (1978); Bede's *A History of the English Church and people* is translated by L Sherley-Price in the Penguin Classics series.

For the medieval period in the Sewingshields area, see the contribution by David Haigh to the report on Sewingshields milecastle by D Haigh and M Savage listed under chapter 6 above.

John Horsley: see Sir George Macdonald, 'John Horsley, scholar and gentleman', *AA* series 4, 10 (1933), 1–57; R G Collingwood 'John Horsley and Hadrian's Wall', *AA* series 4, 15 (1938), 1–42.

On John Clayton: *An account of the Roman antiquities preserved in the museum at Chesters* (compiled by E A Wallis Budge, 1903), 1–25.

10 The Wall today and in the future

Two reports on the Wall and its area are important consultative documents. The first, *Hadrian's Wall*, published in 1976 on behalf of the Countryside Commission by the Dartington Research Trust was a reaction to the visitor explosion on Hadrian's Wall sites in the mid seventies, and formed an attempt to address the problems of the impact of increased leisure activity and tourism on this historic landscape. More recently, a further study by the Countryside Commission *A Strategy for Hadrian's Wall* (1986) sought to form a follow-up to the DART report, and to put those concerns in the context of the pressures on the Wall and its landscape in the 1980s.

Where to visit the Wall

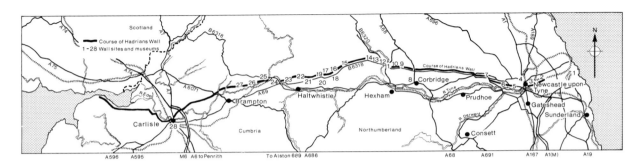

From East to West the major remains of the Wall are:

1. *South Shields fort* (**67, 79–80**)
   Fort established on the south bank of the River Tyne at its mouth. Fort walls, including reconstructed west gate, headquarters and a number of internal granaries/store buildings. Small but interesting museum. (Tyne & Wear Museums)

2. *Wallsend Roman fort*
   The fort at the east end of the Wall. Outline of the fort visible on the ground: remains of gates and the headquarters building. Small museum nearby. (Tyne & Wear Museums/N. Tyneside District Council)

3. *Newcastle Roman fort*
   Traces of buildings belonging to fort of Newcastle beneath castle keep. (Newcastle City Council)

4. *Newcastle, Museum of Antiquities* (**31**)
   In University courtyard, museum containing many sculpted stones from the Wall, reconstruction of temple of Mithras, models of the Wall and selection of finds.

5. *Benwell temple and vallum crossing* (**3, 42**)
   Two separate elements of the surroundings of Benwell fort: the temple of Antenociticus and the causeway across the vallum ditch. (English Heritage)

6. *Denton Turret and Wall*
   Short stretch of Wall and turret 7b. (English Heritage)

7. *Heddon-on-the-Wall*
   A 330 yd (300 m) stretch of Wall. (English Heritage)

8. *Corbridge Roman Site*
   Major town and supply base for Hadrian's Wall area. Remains of 'forum', granaries and military buildings. Large museum with finds from site. (English Heritage)

9. *Planetrees Roman Wall* (**17**)
   Short stretch of Wall incorporating change of width. (English Heritage)

10. *Brunton Turret* (**col pl 10**)
    Stretch of Wall incorporating turret 26b. (English Heritage)

11. *Chesters Bridge abutment* (**23, 24**; **col pl 6**)
East abutment of the Roman bridges carry-
ing the Wall across the River Tyne.
(English Heritage)

12. *Chesters fort and museum* (**15, 32, 35, 54, 59, 60,
61, 84**; **col pl 8, 9**)
Remains of fort (gates, ramparts, headquarters, barracks and commandant's
house) and well-preserved fort bathhouse.
Museum contains rich collection of
material, mainly stones, from many Wall-
sites. (English Heritage)

13. *Black Carts and Limestone corner* (**40, 47, 48**)
Remains of turret 29a, ditch and vallum.
(English Heritage has care of the turret)

14. *Carrawburgh fort and mithraeum* (**64–5**)
Earthworks of fort: small temple of Mithras
outside it. (Fort in private ownership/
English Heritage has care of mithraeum)

15. *Sewingshields Wall* (**51, 81, 85, 86**)
Stretch of Wall of about 2 miles (3 km)
incorporating Milecastles 34 (unexca-
vated) and 35 (excavated), and turrets 33b,
34a and 35a. (English Heritage)

16. *Housesteads Fort* (**34, 37, 38, 39, 58**)
Fort (ramparts, headquarters, commandant's house, latrines, hospital, barracks)
and elements of its surrounding vicus. Visitor centre and small museum. (National
Trust/English Heritage)

17. *Housesteads – Steel Rigg* (**20, 21, 57, 93, 94**)
Wall, milecastles 37, 38 and 39 amid spectacular scenery. (National Trust)

18. *Once Brewed*
Visitor centre for National Park; displays
on Wall-landscape and wildlife. (Northumberland National Park Authority)

19. *Winshields*
Wall, milecastle 40 and turret 40a: the
highest point on the Wall. (English Heritage)

20. *Vindolanda* (**2, 36, 66, 77**)
Fort (ramparts, headquarters, latrine, circular buildings) and extensive settlement
including bathhouse and 'hotel'. Wall
reconstructions. Museum with major collection of material from the site. (English
Heritage has care of fort: remainder Vindolanda Trust)

21. *Cawfields* (**18, 25, col pl 1, 11**)
Stretch of Wall including turret 41a and
milecastle 42. (English Heritage)

22. *Walltown Crags* (**1, 95, 96**)
Wall, including turret 45a. (English Heritage)

23. *Roman Army Museum, Carvoran*
Display on the Roman army in the north:
tableaux and artefacts, visitor centre.

24. *Pottross Burn milecastle*
Remains of milecastle 48, including interior
buildings and layout of walls and gates.
(English Heritage)

25. *Gilsland/Willowford* (**46, col pl 7**)
Substantial stretch of Wall in Gilsland
village and to Willowford farm and crossing of River Irthing, incorporating turrets
48a and 48b, and the east abutment of the
river bridge. (English Heritage)

26. *Birdoswald* (**33, 52, 53, 83, 90**)
Fort (ramparts, gates, granaries) including
substantial stretches of Wall to either side
of it, including milecastle 49, turret 49b.
Small visitor centre/display. (Cumbria
County Council/English Heritage)

27. *Piper Sike, Leahill, Banks turret, Hare Hill*
(**28**)
Five small separate sites, including three
Wall-turrets (nos 51a, 51b, and 52a), a signal
tower (Pike Hill) and one of the highest
surviving fragments of Wall (Hare Hill).
(English Heritage)

28. *Carlisle Museum, Tullie House*
Collection of Roman stones and other finds
from sites at west end of the Wall. (Carlisle
City Council)

Glossary

ala A wing of cavalry in the Roman army — normally of a size, around 512 strong, to occupy a normal auxiliary fort (e.g. Chesters).

auxiliary A Roman soldier in a unit other than a legion.

Broad Wall The module or gauge of Hadrian's Wall as first built, around 10 feet (2.8 m) thick.

century/*centuria* A century of infantry soldiers, normally with a paper strength of between 80–100 men, and commanded by a centurion. A century is the size of unit to be accommodated in a single barrack block.

cohort/*cohors* A unit of infantry (though there were some mixed cohorts) either of single strength — around 500 — or double strength — around 1000 — men strong.

contubernia Single compartments within barrack blocks, suited for the accommodation of 8–10 men and their equipment.

crenellation Battlements along the top of a defensive wall to provide protection for men posted on its top.

forum The centre of a Roman town, incorporating public spaces and market area, normally a large, rectangular open space.

insulae Literally 'islands', the term used for development 'blocks' within a Roman town.

legion/*legio* The elite troops of the Roman army, legions were some 6,000 strong and normally not posted to ordinary 'frontier' duties. They contained specialist units of builders.

milecastle A small walled fortlet incorporating gateways to north and south linked by a central roadway, provided at approximate intervals of one Roman mile for the whole length of Hadrian's Wall. Modern convention numbers these from 0 (at Wallsend) to 80 (at Bowness, Cumbria).

milefortlet A small turf-and-timber fortlet, provided along a stretch of the Cumberland coast west of Hadrian's Wall's western end, and spaced about a Roman mile apart.

Narrow Wall Hadrian's Wall as completed and as in parts rebuilt was not finished to the original Broad Wall specification. Narrow Wall signifies those portions finished to a narrower gauge.

principia The headquarters building within a Roman fort. Set at its centre, this consisted of a courtyard, a lofty hall set across the width of the building, and a series of offices opening off it.

springer The large stone at the top of a gate-jamb from which the gate arch begins.

tail-bedded The term describes facing stones, their external face left relatively free of mortar, but their inner portions (or 'tails') set in the core of a wall for stability.

tribunal A platform within the hall of a headquarters building in a Roman fort.

turf wall The portions of Hadrian's Wall west of the River Irthing at Willowford which were originally built in turf rather than stone.

turret A small rectangular tower, spaced between milecastles at intervals of a third of a Roman mile. Modern convention numbers these in sequence from the east end of the Wall 0a, 0b, 1a, 1b and so on taking their number from the milecastle to their east.

vallum A flat bottomed ditch flanked by mounds running to the south of Hadrian's Wall for much of its length: sometimes close, and sometimes as much as half a mile away, it appears to delimit a military zone.

vexillation A special task-force of Roman troops gathered from several units, or subdi- vided from a unit: normally a portion of a legion.

vicani Collective term for civilians living in the *vicus* next to a Roman fort.

vicus The settlement, normally of civilians, clustered round many Roman forts.

voussoir A wedge-shaped stone forming part of an arch.

wall-walk A footpath or platform provided along the top of a defensive wall.

wing see *ala*.

Index

Illustration numbers are shown in *italics*

140